LIGHT COMES THROUGH

Also by Dzigar Kongtrül

It's Up to You

Light Comes Through

*Buddhist Teachings on Awakening
to Our Natural Intelligence*

Dzigar Kongtrül

SHAMBHALA
BOSTON & LONDON
2008

SHAMBHALA PUBLICATIONS, INC.
Horticultural Hall
300 Massachusetts Avenue
Boston, Massachusetts 02115
www.shambhala.com

9 8 7 6 5 4 3 2 1

First Edition

Printed in the United States of America

⊗ This edition is printed on acid-free paper that meets
the American National Standards Institute z39.48 Standard.

Distributed in the United States by Random House, Inc.,
and in Canada by Random House of Canada Ltd

Designed by Jeff Baker

Library of Congress Cataloging-in-Publication Data

Kongtrül, Dzigar.
Light comes through: Buddhist teachings on awakening to our natural
intelligence / Dzigar Kongtrül.
p. cm.
ISBN 978-1-59030-567-6 (hardcover: alk. paper)
1. Religious life—Buddhism. 2. Buddhism—Doctrines. I. Title.
BQ4302.K675 2008
294.3'444—dc22
2007042006

CONTENTS

Editor's Preface   *vii*

Acknowledgments   *xi*

Introduction   *xiii*

PART ONE: THE FIVE SELF-CENTERED EMOTIONS

1. Self-Clinging: The Juice of Self-Centered Emotions   3

2. Guilty as Charged!: A Case against Jealousy   9

3. The Other Side of the Fence:
   A Case against Aggression   17

4. Invisible Strings: A Case against Attachment   29

5. Entering the Circle of Dogs:
   A Case against Arrogance   39

6. Connecting Seed and Fruit: A Case against Stupidity   47

PART TWO: WORKING WITH OTHERS

7. The *Lenchak* Dynamic: Not a Healthy Kind of Love   55

8. Part of the Equation: No Room for Indifference   65

9. Putting Others in the Center:
   The Fundamental Principle   69

10. Faith: Opening the Shutters   75

11. Working with a Teacher: Not a One-hand Clap   81

12. Devotion and Lineage:
    From the Womb of the Mother   89

PART THREE: TEACHINGS ON EMPTINESS

13. Mere Appearance: Thinking like an Elephant   97

14. The Haunted Dominion of the Mind:
    Shaken from Within   103

15. The "Unfindability" of Phenomena:
    Disassembling Delusion   113

16. Light Comes Through: Potential and Entirety   119

Recommended Reading   123

Mangala Shri Bhuti Centers   125

EDITOR'S PREFACE

In the West we have a long history of searching for truth in the realms of science, art, and philosophy. Yet we maintain a clear distinction between intellectual pursuit and matters of the heart. We don't have a strong tradition that reconciles faith and spirituality with direct investigation. Generally, faith and feeling require acceptance, not inquiry. Mind is reserved for empirical matters, while the heart just "knows" through intuition.

Ask someone from the West, "Where is the mind?" Most often that person will point to their head. Ask the same person, "Where is the heart?"—the place they feel things—and they will point to their chest. We don't find this in all cultures. A Tibetan, for instance, will not separate mind and heart in the same manner. If you ask a Tibetan to locate mind, they will most likely point to their chest.

The Tibetan term *nyingje,* or "compassion," for instance, refers to both thought and feeling. *Changchub kyi sem* can translate as either the "mind" or "heart" of enlightenment. If we don't understand the interdependence of heart and mind, we can't use either to its fullest potential. When we separate clear reasoning from experience, our emotional and conceptual life runs amok. If we get pedantic in our views, we can't make them practical.

In truth, beyond cultural interpretation, we can't actually separate experience from awareness—heart and mind are linked in that experience and awareness arise in dependence upon one another. For instance, we can't experience physical or emotional feelings devoid of cognition. Similarly, we can't speak of cognition without an object, be it an emotion, thought, or thing. When we engage mind through a process of subjective inquiry, we naturally include our emotional, spiritual, physical, and conceptual life.

This is done in a particular way on the Buddhist path. It is not a psychological approach that attempts to make "sense" of experience by tracing it back to its source. It does not attempt to reify experience or impute any conceptual meaning upon anything whatsoever. The point is to have a fresh and immediate look at experience like a child exploring the phenomenal world and learning how it works. Children learn from playful inquiry and immediate engagement with the world around them: the hotness of fire, the breakable-ness of objects, the sweetness of candy, and the pain of falling down.

The purpose of all study, contemplation, and meditation on the Buddhist path is to wear away ignorance—this happens from learning what gives rise to confusion and what liberates. Wearing away ignorance requires effort. We have rigorously established our delusion, and it will likewise take some effort to disassemble it. The author of this book, Dzigar Kongtrül, on one occasion, described how as a young scholar he used to cover his head with his meditation shawl and engage, for hours, in deep contemplation on such topics as impermanence, *bodhichitta*, and emptiness.

This deep and personal practice of breaking down ignorance through the contemplation of Dharma transforms the mind. More than an accumulation of knowledge, it is a method that guides us toward direct understanding. For instance, it does not serve us to simply proclaim, "Everything is impermanent!" as we continue to grasp onto our youth, beauty, and possessions anyway. The purpose of reasoning and contemplation is to arrive at experiential truth. Our understanding is not dry and impersonal, as some may assume, because it is not divorced from our own living experience. Approaching our mind in this way has a freeing and clarifying effect, which lets the light of our natural intelligence shine through the confusion that ordinarily binds us.

Light Comes Through is a tribute to the potential of reasoning mind and what can happen when it fortuitously discovers the Buddhist path. In it Kongtrül engages an exploration of basic human experiences beginning with the five disturbing, self-centered emotions: attachment, aggression, stupidity, jealousy, and pride. He moves on to explore human relationships and concludes with the subtlest use of the reasoning mind—its ability to analyze the nature of reality itself. The beauty of the buddhadharma is that it is inclusive: we need not reject or fabricate experience, but instead we can engage our lives in ways that bring heart and mind together in the most intimate way.

—*Elizabeth Mattis-Namgyel*

ACKNOWLEDGMENTS

My wife, Elizabeth, has worked on this volume with so much wisdom and precision, finding the language to accurately and eloquently convey my interest and intentions to a wider audience. If it were not for her, *Light Comes Through* would not be the book that it is. I must completely acknowledge her devotion and dedication to the Dharma, the lineage, and to the benefit of beings, all of which shine through in her work. I would like to also acknowledge Sasha Meyerowitz for his part in the editing process and for talking through the topics. My gratitude goes to Emily Bower for her insights into the structure and logic of the whole and to Hazel Berholz for her elegant cover design. Finally, no book can begin without the effort of the transcribers, whom I warmly thank.

—Dzigar Kongtrül

INTRODUCTION

Anything and everything can arise in the mind. This is either good news or not such good news, depending on how we look at it. On one hand, it means anything and everything is possible. On the other hand, if we possess no understanding of mind and how it works, we will be—as the traditional example describes—like someone without limbs trying to ride a wild, blind horse. We will not be able to reign in the mind, and so the mind will never serve us—it will never take us where we want to go.

The Buddhist teachings address the mind: how it functions and how we can shape the mind so that it can serve us. If we don't learn how to shape the mind, the mind will continue to shape itself. Rather than training in wisdom, it will train and habituate itself against our will, our intentions, our better judgments—it will do as it fancies. We already know how much we suffer from our habits. It is amazing how resilient we are as human beings: we suffer over and over again but just keep on going!

In order to shape the mind, to make it work for us, we need to rely on an aspect of mind itself—an aspect we can call our natural intelligence. We may sometimes wonder where to find our natural intelligence—or if we even have any at all. But the fact is, in ordinary, everyday ways, we utilize our natural intelligence all of the time. Without it, we would lack the ability to make basic decisions and to discriminate between things that will help or hinder us. We rely on it while rummaging through our closets in the morning looking for the perfect thing to wear.

We base all our ethical principles upon it. Natural intelligence weighs all the pros and cons; it organizes and analyzes. It has the capacity to see the interdependent connection of various elements and how they function together. And it searches for happiness and meaning . . . even if it sometimes can't find them. Without this essential tool it is doubtful we would get anything done at all. And any notion of enlightenment, most certainly, would be out of the question.

The *buddhadharma* harnesses the power of natural intelligence in a unique way. As we encounter mind's raw, unprocessed conceptual activity, the teachings encourage us to utilize our natural intelligence to look dispassionately at mind and emotions and sort through our confusion and ignorance; in this way we uncover our innate wisdom and clarity. The Buddhist teachings affirm this natural gift and also challenge us: "Analyze! See if this isn't true." Everything we need to move forward is right here.

IMAGINE A VAGUE ENLIGHTENMENT

It takes some time to refine the mind through this process of exploration. We may have some resistance to using conceptual mind—thinking mind—in this way. The prospect of investigating mind may not fit the description we have of a spiritual path—it may seem too analytical, too bookish or precise. We may prefer to keep our notion of spirituality vague and open-ended. We may wish to reach for a nonconceptual state absent of thought. Or we may only select spiritual ideas we feel comfortable with instead of exploring what we don't understand. In this way, we maintain a more romantic view of spirituality—one that will make us feel good and that is separate from our ordinary, sometimes troubled life, the life we are trying to break free of. If we keep things a little abstract, we can continue in our usual ways. We can keep all of our options open, and we won't have to worry about shaking off old habits. Our self-image remains intact—just as we like. But try to imagine a vague enlightenment: What might that be like?

And while we are waiting for our vague enlightenment, what should we do with our conceptual mind, which seems to churn mindlessly 99.99 percent of the time, day and night? Even in the seclusion of retreat, cut off from the stimuli of everyday life, the mind never stops chatting away. And with nothing to distract us, the volume seems louder than ever. If we try to disregard the conceptual mind or to wait for it to go away so that we can finally attain enlightenment, we will be waiting forever.

Since our experience of both happiness and pain depends upon the mind, wouldn't it make sense to learn how it works? Demystifying the relationship we have with our mind, our thoughts and emotions, is the essence of the Buddhist teachings. It is like switching on the light in a dark room: no matter how long a room has remained in a state of darkness, once we turn on the light, everything is illuminated.

A fully illuminated mind doesn't need shaping at all. There are no dark corners and nothing to fear. Mind in its entirety never wavers from its fundamentally free and unobstructed state. All the qualities of wisdom and compassion naturally preside within it. Much of the time, because the mind is obscured by its own bewilderment, we experience only a fraction of its true potential. This fraction of our potential reveals itself to us as our natural intelligence—it is the call of the entirety of our buddha nature. Light comes through, and instinctually we want to respond to it—to reach for its source.

A fully illuminated mind sees through conceptual mind itself. In other words, we shape the conceptual mind to ultimately transcend it—to uncover its source. But make no mistake about it, until we have stability in this kind of direct experience, the clarity of our natural intelligence remains our greatest support. This is particularly true now in this age of lessening faith and increasing confusion. We so often encounter meditators who, after twenty years of practice, still have trouble working with their mind and emotions and are still perplexed by their relationships with others.

Through open and playful inquiry, we can increase our understanding of how to use the mind, how to question our experience through internal dialogue, and how to analyze the many aspects of life that usually seem to resist analysis. As we do this, we find that the truth naturally reveals itself to us—as the hotness of fire reveals itself to us when we touch it or the day reveals itself to us when we wake up in the morning. Our mind, our most precious natural resource, rather than posing a threat, will take us where we want to go.

Part One

THE FIVE
SELF-CENTERED
EMOTIONS

Self-Clinging

The Juice of Self-Centered Emotions

The reason we study and practice the *buddhadharma* is to learn how to work with our minds. We need to work with our minds particularly during difficult times, when our mind is not friendly, when it frightens us to the point that we would rather not even associate with it. Dharma teaches us how to look at our mind and familiarize ourselves with how it works. We learn what its patterns are, how it goes out of control and threatens us as well as others. In essence, Dharma cultivates our intelligence. It allows an intelligent person to come out from behind the habits, impulses, and reactions that normally dominate the mind. Then when the momentum and power of our "mind gone wild" begin to stir, we don't feel like a feather in the wind.

In Buddhism, we speak a lot about the false belief in an ego or self and how clinging to that self creates suffering. Sometimes the notion of clinging to the self may seem abstract. What does it feel like when we cling to the self? It is important to be able to identify that experience. The belief in the self that we cling to needs to be examined through analytical meditation and clear thinking. We can directly examine the false belief in a self by looking at the raw, visceral experience of self-clinging and the suffering it produces. In Tibetan, this clinging is called *shenpa*. One cannot separate shenpa from ego-clinging; they are different aspects of the same thing. But if we were to distinguish them, we would say that shenpa is the energy and momentum of ego-clinging. Shenpa drives our habits, impulses, and reactions. We must expose shenpa to our intelligence in order to see through its momentum.

In English, shenpa is generally translated as "attachment." But we cannot equate shenpa with just one term. Rather shenpa is a pervasive discomfort; it is the experience of "I, me, and mine" and all the wants, needs, aversions, hopes, and fears that come out of that. In this way, shenpa is found in attachment and aversion, stupidity, pride, and jealousy. The discomfort of shenpa can be vague and subtle, as one student described, like "having a stone in your shoe" or "a sour note that plays throughout the day." Or, when ego is strongly challenged, we experience shenpa as the painful charge in the five negative emotions. Shenpa is the juice of our ego.

Shenpa comes alive whenever there is a strong sense of self-importance. We think of everything in terms of what we want in or out of our lives, what will help or hinder us, and what we hope and fear. We struggle to fix and maintain the world according to our preferences. This is burdensome and impossible and leaves us vulnerable to tremendous suffering. Even if our emotions are not wild and crazy, our internal struggle, our sense of not being content and at peace, will remain strong. Shenpa defines the quality of our emotional life, and not in positive way. It leaves us with only two choices in relating to our emotions: we can either reject or vent.

When through shenpa we reject or suppress our emotions, it is just a question of how tight a lid we can put on the pressure cooker. If the cooker keeps cooking, then no matter how heavy the lid and how tight the seal, at some point it will blow up. And even if it doesn't blow up, the food inside will be overcooked. Suppression is a form of violence toward ourselves, where we automatically judge our experience to be negative and our emotions to be bad, and then identify with them in a personal way. Wherever there is aversion, a story line is produced. Rejecting what arises is an expression of shenpa, which is always based on preferences aimed at cherishing and protecting the self. It leaves us with bitter feelings and difficulties that haunt us.

Instead of suppressing, the other side of the coin is to vent. Something is bugging us, an emotional storm is brewing, and right away we're ready to get into the ring with our gloves on. In the beginning of that momentum, there's even a driving force of excitement, the excitement of seeing who will win. And the consequences don't seem so bad. But if we go through this several times a day, with parents, spouses, children, with the ones we are supposed to love and care for, or even with just our own minds, then it wears us out and brings relationships to a painful point. So indulging doesn't serve us in the end, although it may have the appearance of facing the truth. But in fact, venting our emotions is just another way of trying to get rid of them.

Both rejecting and indulging in our experience indicate that somehow we don't understand the nature of our own minds and emotions, that we are intimidated by our experience in some way and are bound by the preferences of our self-importance. We have to familiarize ourselves with the mechanisms and consequences of shenpa and self-importance in order to see through them. Then they will no longer have a hold on us.

At the monastery near where I grew up there used to be a snow-lion dance every year. We children used to get excited but also afraid because we knew at the end the lions would jump up on us and terrify us. As we grew older and saw the dance year after year, the fear began to vanish. The dance had not changed, but our minds had matured, because we understood that the snow lions were just monks wearing masks. This understanding liberated us from fear.

In a similar way, unmasking the nature of our shenpa and self-importance places us on the path to peace. To expose shenpa to our intelligence means to bring it out of the hidden, dark corners of our minds into the light of our awareness. The key in this process is to look at our habits, impulses, and emotions without judgment. You can call this confession practice because you are accepting the more challenging aspects of mind, rather than trying to hide or manipulate them; you can call it courage; you can call it being honest—whatever you label it, it has a freeing quality. The underlying pain of shenpa begins to melt like ice when exposed to the warmth of our awareness. Acceptance replaces the struggle of rejection and indulgence. Appreciation for the true character of our minds grows.

The main attitude on the path to peace is to accept whatever our experience brings. When we speak of not indulging or not suppressing, it doesn't mean we don't use our discriminating intelligence. It simply means we are not reacting from a vague or fearful state where that intelligence is enslaved by our hopes and fears.

Coming from a clear vantage point, we know why we make the decisions we make and where we intend to go with our paths and lives, rather than being swept away by our shenpa. Even in the midst of an emotional storm, when our shenpa is strongly activated, we need not see our habitual reactions as problems in themselves. The problem all along has been our fear and lack of clarity. When we see clearly, we can understand that shenpa, ego, and the emotions ego generates are all part of the human mind, and we can work with them. Relating to emotions without the rejection and indulgence of shenpa, we can freely examine them because they are no longer personal. This is emotional intelligence, a sign that our mind is maturing as a practitioner. We can see for ourselves how emotional intelligence clears up not only our relation with our own mind but also our relationships with others. This will bring stability and peace into our lives.

2

Guilty as Charged!

A Case against Jealousy

Buddhist texts traditionally list the five disturbing emotions beginning with attachment and then move on to aggression, stupidity, jealousy, and arrogance. But here I'd like to start with jealousy because it is the most obvious, ridiculous, and embarrassing of all the emotions, which makes it easier to overcome. If we practice working with jealousy first, we will have more confidence in working with the subtlety of the other emotions later.

The jealous mind wants what others have, be it physical attributes, wealth, intelligence, someone else's spouse, their job, status, spiritual accomplishments, and so on. Because it focuses on what it doesn't have, it feels impoverished and discontent all the time. When we are possessed by jealousy, it is as if something were lacking in our very existence—something that someone else has. Jealousy is a comparative dynamic that causes us to resent others. We resent their positive attributes and continually search for their weaknesses: "Why do *they* possess those attributes that should belong to *me!*"

The jealous mind is gross and obvious. Not only do we lose respect for ourselves when we feel jealous, but everyone else loses respect for us too. We feel exposed like a worm whose rock has been overturned. As much as we want to hide, we lose face. In this way, the grossness of jealousy has some value—nothing is hidden, so we can see it and then try to overcome it . . . or at least have a good laugh.

Of all the emotions, jealousy is the most crass and easy to identify. Because comparing with others is what jealousy likes to do best, let's compare jealousy with the other negative emotions to see how we can identify it: One could easily argue that *aggression,* not jealousy, is the grossest emotion of all because aggression often expresses itself with intensity. But aggression can be subtle. We can easily convince ourselves that we have good reason to be angry. It takes a much deeper and subtler level of strength and conviction in nonviolence to give up aggression completely. *Attachments* are deep rooted and there are so many of them. Furthermore, our attachments are so often mixed with caring feelings and pleasure that we find it difficult emotionally to even entertain the thought of giving them up. The *arrogant* mind is more slippery than jealousy. We often mistake arrogance for the strength that keeps us from buckling under our weaknesses. There is a fine line between arrogance and self-confidence. And last but not least is *stupidity.* Stupidity is the hardest emotion to detect of them all because our minds are so shrouded in habitual patterns. It sits on the sidelines never questioning anything, so the whole mechanism of jealousy just keeps operating. But with jealousy what you see is what you get. It can't even maintain a false sense of self-esteem like all the other emotions can.

Beneath all of this crassness is the self-cherishing ego, backing jealousy up every step of the way. But at the same time, ego doesn't approve—jealousy is just too embarrassing. Ego tries to reject the idea that such a thing could possibly be a part of its "stainless" mental stream. Ego's reaction is like someone getting drunk and acting stupid at an office party and then trying to back up their foolish conduct with logic and reason the next morning at work. It just doesn't go over. When we interrogate it, jealousy breaks down before it reaches the witness stand. Guilty as charged!

The Practice of Rejoicing

Okay, we confess, jealousy is clumsy . . . and not only because it assaults our sense of vanity. We have to admit that it causes pain, that it prevents us from appreciating our own life and gets in between our relationships with others in an unwholesome way. But to stop here would not be enough. Like all emotions, jealousy is habitual, which means that even though we have investigated the harm it can do and the merits of overcoming it— even if we are completely convinced—it will still rise up again out of habit. What we need now is a very strong antidote, and the antidote to jealousy is the practice of rejoicing.

Rejoicing is simply feeling happy when something fortunate or beneficial happens to someone other than ourselves. Imagine going to a football match. Everyone cheers for their team. If someone makes a goal, the whole team jumps up and down and hugs each other. Sometimes they carry the player that scored on their shoulders. Even the most macho guy on the team has tears in his eyes. Everyone in the stands rises up yelling and waving flags—elated, rejoicing because of this player's accomplishment. This person's accomplishment has become their accomplishment too.

We can find so many ways to rejoice and so many things to rejoice in. Rejoicing practice is like this: a little bit of labor, but much merit. In other words, we simply share in the joy of others' virtue, which is a virtuous act in itself. When someone becomes a vegetarian or donates money to a charitable organization, we can rejoice. We can rejoice in the virtue of people who have put their life on the line to help others, the Good Samaritan we hear about on the news. We can rejoice in the spiritual accomplishments of others, too. We can rejoice in the realization of the buddhas and bodhisattvas and in the liberation of the arhats.*

We can also rejoice in the beauty of the world and the fact that others have the merit to enjoy it. We can rejoice when the sun comes up in the morning and warms an entire valley and all the beings in it, or when the rain falls, providing water for the crops. We can rejoice in the physical abilities of others—that a bird can fly or that a fish can swim, things that we can only imagine doing ourselves. A friend of mine was in a car accident and injured his neck. He suffered a great deal from this and couldn't move about freely. One day he was watching a flock of swans swimming in a lake on TV. He noticed how agile their necks were, how they moved about with so much ease, grace, and flexibility . . . and, without even thinking about it, he began to rejoice in their freedom of movement. At that moment he experienced a deep sense of joy that took him beyond the concerns he had for his own condition.

We need to ask ourselves, "Why does it always have to be *my* joy? Why is it so hard to delight in the joy of others?" Why, after sitting in front of the TV version of how things should be, do we need to think, "Why isn't it like that for me?" We feel deprived when we indulge in this kind of comparison. We feel like we are missing out on the "cheese"—all the goodies this world has to offer. These days there is so much competitiveness,

---

*A Buddhist saint who has fully awakened to selflessness and has eradicated all passions and desires.

people feel squeezed and impoverished no matter how much they have. This is because there is not an inner sense of richness. Ages ago one gold coin would make someone feel rich. Now even a million dollars won't do. Children have a room full of toys but get easily bored. We can remedy all of this through the practice of rejoicing.

Generally, we love praise when it comes in our direction. We rejoice in every occasion we can of being happy with ourselves. But when we have the chance to be happy for others, why reject that? We say, "Peace on earth, good will toward men" and "Love thy neighbor." Furthermore, some of us take the bodhisattva vow to attain enlightenment for the benefit of all beings. So how do we justify getting irritated when others obtain a little bit of happiness, a little bit of accomplishment, in this world where happiness is so ephemeral and so hard to obtain? We should feel relieved in the same way parents feel relieved when their children are able to stand on their own two feet.

The mean-spiritedness of jealousy will not lead anyone to enlightenment. The logic of jealousy exposes all our stupidity and shows the inconsistency in our thinking. So consider the practice of rejoicing. It removes any trace of "I, me, and mine" from our mind streams. When we rejoice in the well-being of others, we break free of that subtle self-absorption that threatens us from inside. We will no longer be willing to get knocked down by jealousy—that ridiculous emotion! We will begin to see the freeing effects of rejoicing and the blessing of it. The positivity of rejoicing practice releases within us the qualities of intelligence, selflessness, generosity, patience, strength, and good-heartedness. How can we feel the pain of jealousy in the midst of this abundance of good qualities?

Obviously, this is something that won't make any sense to us unless we have the liberating experience that comes from actually rejoicing ourselves. In the beginning stages of counter-acting jealousy, we may need to force the practice of rejoicing upon it. Of course, we need good reasons for doing this; other-wise, we won't get motivated. Many people might find the idea of forcing to be artificial. Unfortunately, to go with what comes naturally to us usually means falling prey to our emotions, so we need to apply a strong remedy by modifying our behavior, which in turn modifies our thoughts and emotions. We use this practice to deliberately shape the mind to work for us.

Cultivating Wealth through Pennies

Sometimes people say that they find it difficult to rejoice in the temporal happiness of samsara.* When we hear, for example, that someone has purchased a $35 million house, it may rub against some of our principles. We might think about the many trees that had to be cut down and all the natural shrubs, wild-flowers, and animals that were cleared from the property. And were their $35 million clean? Where did that money come from anyway? Why can't they spend that money on something less selfish, on charity perhaps? Furthermore, we may have certain value judgments about people who live such extravagant lifestyles. Sometimes these kinds of questions and attitudes come up around rejoicing practice. How do we rejoice in the temporal happiness of samsara when in truth we see so much pain, inequality, and injustice?

When we look around at the world, we must remember that we are all part of the equation of suffering. No one lives in iso-lation. From the food we eat to the clothes we wear to the fuel we fill our cars with, we depend on so many others. In fact, we

*The world of confusion created by ignorance and characterized by suffering.

owe a tremendous debt to others. No matter how hard we try—even if we sell our car and take the bus instead—this will always be the case. Our lives are interrelated with others' and we indirectly contribute to both their joy and suffering. Although we may live in an ethical and thoughtful manner, serving others in any way we can, our role in the pervasiveness of suffering is a truth we must accept. Knowing this, we can leave our principles outside the door.

Others' happiness is not a matter of principle. In fact, our principles are a stumbling block to the whole idea of rejoicing. Rejoicing is a matter of the heart. Although living beings often don't know the causes and conditions that give rise to happiness and sometimes even confuse suffering with pleasure, in their hearts they value the rare and fleeting experience of happiness over anything else.

To rejoice in others' happiness without any preferences of our own shows that we understand that the longing for happiness is the same for all beings. We can rejoice in their temporal happiness, which has come from their accumulation of merit. When we recognize the quality of happiness in others—when we see someone genuinely smile or laugh or see a glimmer of brightness in their eyes—we can rejoice. When they obtain something they want or need, whatever it may be, we have an opportunity to practice rejoicing. Beings long for all kinds of things, some of which we might not want ourselves—but that doesn't matter. The important thing is that, if only for a single moment, it has brought them some happiness.

By practicing rejoicing we can go far beyond counteracting jealousy. Rejoicing introduces us to the wealth of the world. With this practice, we might feel more fulfillment than we would with having all the riches of the world drop right into our very lap. We start to notice the goodness in others, beginning with their inherent longing for happiness. Not a moment goes by that we can't rejoice in the potential of mind or in the beauty around us. Even one moment of rejoicing in others' happiness and merit can sustain us for the entire day. It is like cultivating wealth through pennies. We are walking down the street, and we see something glimmering in the gutter. We pick it up—a penny! Then we start to look around, and we see more. Soon the streets are so full of pennies, our pockets can't even hold them all.

3

The Other Side of the Fence

A Case against Aggression

You are at a party and there are beautiful people, surround-
ings, and laughter. The music is good too. Suddenly someone gets angry and throws a glass of champagne. It ruins the
whole show—even the dog leaves the room. When someone
gets angry, it effects the whole environment like an unpleasant
odor that everyone has to smell. And, as our mental states are
often quite fragile, it disturbs people's minds. But it disturbs the
person who gets angry more than anyone else.

When we get angry, we lose the dignity of our intelligence.
We become a stranger to pleasure. Others stay away from us,
and we are left alone with our mind and all the residue that
comes from our angry reaction. We feel vulnerable to the core,
not because something happened outside, but rather because
we've lost trust in our ability to respond to situations in a sane
and reasonable way.

Most people don't consider themselves violent or aggressive. Moreover, most of us condemn the violence we hear about
in the news or witness around us. But aggression expresses itself
in many, often subtle, ways. We may not necessarily lash out
when we are aggressive. We may just have a sour or distrustful
attitude toward others in such a way that we no longer keep

them in the realm of our care. We may suspect someone is angry at us: "He didn't say a word when he saw me. What did I do to deserve that?" The imaginary scenarios we create seem to proliferate on their own. Because we no longer trust this person, we take away their "ally status" and put him or her on the other side of the fence. Whether we are "spitting fire" or quietly harboring animosity, aggressive mind is always engaged in rejecting with a sense of aversion.

We may even have an external reason for our suspicion that someone is against us or wants to bring us down. Someone we considered a friend may no longer back us in some way. This happens. We may need to use our critical intelligence and remove ourselves from a harmful situation or take care in terms of relating to certain individuals. We may even need to speak out against something that has potentially harmful consequences for a larger group of people, a nation, or the world at large. But proceed with caution: Sometimes aggression moves in. And when it does, we often mistake it for discerning intelligence or our instinct for expressing generosity and care or our longing to better the world around us. The reason for this is that anger gives the illusion of clarity. A certain strength arises when we have an opinion and we know where we stand.

The difference between the clarity we believe we have when angry and the clarity that results from actually seeing clearly is that aggression has its own narrow logic, which does not take into account the deeper level of causes and conditions that surround each situation. Because it has no foresight or perspective, the aggressive mind doesn't see any reason to hold back; it is only concerned with preserving the sense of self it seems to be working for. It doesn't think about peace or disturbance, benefit or harm, so it does not try to reroute itself in an emotionally positive direction. Aggression fixes its logic on the wrongness of other and always possesses the distinctive feature of aversion. We see that aggression results, to some degree or another, in our not responding well to situations. We lose our poise and dignity and get all keyed up like a nervous little dog barking and jumping around, trying to intimidate others. We lose our ability for reasonable discernment, which we regain only after our anger has subsided. But by this time it is too late. We've created a mess, and we feel shredded.

Needless to say, when we expel others from the realm of our care, we ignore our bodhisattva vow. When we take the bodhisattva vow, does it say, "May all beings find perfect happiness . . . except all politicians and my ex"? Do we leave out terrorists; dictators; big, hairy spiders; and everyone that irritates us? When we put anyone on the other side of the fence, we lose our foundation for seeing clearly and acting for the welfare of self and others. Instead, we begin to experience a lot of anxiety and fear. We can see that the people who have the most aggression are the most paranoid of all. Fear and paranoia come with aggression because, when we have made a separation between ourselves and others, we have, in effect, created enemies. This is a form of violence.

Of course, we can come up with all sorts of scenarios to justify our aggression. They may be logical and fair. . . . We may even be "right"; after all, one hundred people back us up on this! So we throw in the towel and say, "I can't take it anymore—I've had it!" Anger seems reasonable when we feel threatened. As it's said, "anger comes in the guise of a friend"—righteous and protective and with airtight logic. Someone or something else is always responsible. But this logic only blinds us, and we get hit hard with our own fear and aggression instead. So what good does this do even if we win?

EGO'S EMPIRE

The pain and anxiety we experience in our lives are in equal measure to the size of our self-importance. Our attachment to self is at the center of ego's world—ego's empire. We want the best for ourselves and all those we associate with ourselves. All that we include as part of me and mine is ego's domain. Of course, this is unstable and changing all the time. Someone might say, "Oh, I love your children," so they're in. Someone doesn't back you on a project or puts down your country—they're out. In the traditional Tibetan Buddhist teachings, those we associate with ourselves usually include our friends and family. When a loved one is ill, we may find it more unbearable than if we fell ill ourselves. But oddly, we often have less tolerance for those closest to us. This shows how bewildered our mind can be.

Meanwhile, we want happiness and do everything we can to avoid suffering. We long for the material goodies this world has to offer but then fear losing or not being able to obtain them. We hope for sweet praise to reach our tender ears but fear criticism and disapproval. We want recognition and fame, and dread ordinariness and obscurity. The preoccupations we have with our various hopes and fears fill our whole day. We have anxieties of not getting what we want, with so many people in the way, and a readiness to leap into aggression when we don't. Let me tell you, this is not helpful! We hold tight to our empire, which only means more aggression for us.

As for our adversaries—those we put on the other side of the fence—we secretly wish for them not to succeed or accumulate wealth or do well. When we hear they are happy, we might say, "What wonderful news!" but it does not sit well inside. When something unfortunate happens to them, we feel a sense of relief. Conversely, when we hear, for example, that the stock portfolio of someone we don't like has gone up, it hits us hard in the gut. If someone likes this person, we make a special point of exposing all of our adversary's faults by saying something negative. We try to give our naive friend a little bit of "truth."

In our attempt to secure ego's empire, we must wrestle with the world and all its unpredictability. We have so much less control than we would like. All our hopes, fears, and preferences stir up feelings of insecurity within us and feed our mental unrest and aggression. The way we feed our mental unrest is often subtle. We may find ourselves sitting across the dinner table from our spouse, casually venting some insecurities about the day's events: "He is mad at me. . . . She is not behind me. . . . I don't like the way he . . ." Letting our minds wander into negative thinking ruptures our peace of mind. It's a dangerous direction to let our minds move in.

Self-Aggression

Our aggression can point outwardly toward external objects, or it can fix on our inner life of thoughts and emotions. When we sit to practice meditation, we may find it hard to face what's "in there." All sorts of undesirable sensations and thoughts arise. Our response? "This is bad . . . very bad indeed. I need to cut this. I need to get rid of this. I'm so intense!" Our inner life does not often fit the image of ourselves that we try to maintain. Sometimes we doubt the possibility of ever having a positive relation to this self at all. Guilt and aversion arise as yet another form of aggression—the rejection of how we see ourselves, how we feel, what we think.

The world is what it is; we have to face what is happening around us, our relationships, or just whatever goes on in our own mind. We cannot expect it all to go away. We have to be practical; otherwise, we just create further suffering for ourselves. Much of the time, we can't resist the temptation of sorting things out with our emotions. When neuroses and negative thoughts arise, we react by either suppressing or venting them—both responses, of course, aimed at trying to get rid of unwanted experiences.

THE PRACTICE OF NONVIOLENCE

On the Buddhist path, rather than trying to protect ourselves from our own mind, we actively investigate mind in order to understand how it works. We often have to be quite critical of our habits. We have to look at our faults, including our aggression. We have to examine our neuroses. There is research to be done! If we respond with revulsion toward our mind and its activities, this inquiry cannot take place. We need to understand the mechanics of aggression and learn to reflect in a nonjudgmental way. We may be hard on ourselves, thinking we have "anger-management problems" or calling ourselves "a lost cause." But in this way, we just sidestep really looking. We need to look at the mind without judgments of good or bad. At the same time, we need to understand how both good and bad are defined by virtue of how they function to create happiness and pain. In other words, we need to sort things out with wisdom mind and bring them into review.

There is much to appreciate in ourselves and our minds—even in being "messed up." The more we know, the more we can resolve; while the more we reject, the more we alienate ourselves from our experience. If we are truly to abandon something, we should do so with wisdom rather than aggression or fear. If only we knew how to bring our difficulties into the light of our intelligence.

All the Buddha's teachings find roots in nonviolence: non-violence toward others, nonviolence toward ourselves, and non-violence even toward negative emotions. It is important that we have a taste of the peace that comes from nonaggression. The dualistic tendency to push things away poses the biggest problem for us. We have so many wants and "unwants" . . . but how wonderful—there is room for all. When we begin to understand our minds' habits, we have the leverage to slowly and steadily outsmart them.

The famous Tibetan meditator Geshe Ben said that his only practice was to watch his self-importance bloat up and then crumble down again and again. Seeing how it made his mind freer and freer every time it crumbled brought meaning and pleasure to his life. In fact, it was his life's passion. His is an example of a genuinely nonviolent attitude toward his own mind and experience. We should study such examples and let them rub off on us. Even just admiring someone who lives this way can undermine our addiction to our emotions. We can study his or her attitudes, wisdom, and broad-mindedness. Bodhisattvas engage in the practical discipline of nonviolence toward their own minds and the world around them. They have simply decided to resort to wisdom instead of aggression.

His Holiness the Dalai Lama, I'm certain, considers all the people of the world as his friends. We often see pictures of him in books and magazines holding someone's hand tightly—as if they have been buddies for his entire life. When we listen to his speech or see him with others, his compassion and inclusiveness strike us. Although China still occupies Tibet, it is hard not to notice that His Holiness continues to refer to the Chinese people as his brothers and sisters rather than putting them on the other side of the fence. His example alone teaches us how to practice nonviolence. It shows us that whoever practices nonviolence not only pacifies his or her own mind but also everyone around him. Kindness naturally provides others with a way to respond that is free of aggression and hatred. Mahatma Gandhi said that when you are able to respond to another's aggression nonviolently, that person softens and they are able to self-reflect. Acting upon these principles, the Indian people won independence from the British Empire. Through the practice of nonviolence, we can surely gain independence from our own afflictions.

We may think that nonviolence is a meek, passive, or naive response to the wrongdoings in the world. In relationships, we fear that, if we don't respond aggressively, we will be victimized or taken advantage of. We would rather settle our scores through fighting back in order to preserve our sense of dignity and strength. But nonviolence does not fall into the extremes of either aggression or passivity. Nonviolence is a path of total engagement.

The great practitioners of nonviolence have never turned their heads or shrunk away from their own or others' suffering. Knowing the downfalls of aggression, they have been able to respond with wisdom and broad-mindedness. This type of wisdom and courage grows from our commitment to understanding our own mind and reactions and the causes and results of our actions. We develop the ability to accurately read and respond to the world around us without rejecting it. This is the practice of nonviolence. Of course this takes some maturity. We really need to cultivate this kind of maturity.

POSITIVE DISGUST

Normally we have so little control over our emotions—and we feel our vulnerability as a tight knot in our chests. People talk

about needing armor, particularly around their chests, to protect themselves when they go to war. Even bugs have shells to
protect themselves. But no physical armor can protect us from
what disturbs us inside. We cannot hide ourselves in a box in
order to insulate ourselves from our own minds. The only real
protection we have is the practice of nonviolence.

In Tibetan, the term for nonviolence is *tseme zopa. Zopa* is
translated as patience, tolerance, or endurance. Inherent in *zopa*
is a feeling of positive disgust, or renunciation, that comes from
knowing the negative result of anger. This disgust is similar to
the disgust we might experience from eating the same greasy
food again and again, day after day. Through constantly getting
burnt by our own aggression, we will lose our taste for anything
that feeds it and instead turn toward the virtues of practicing
patience. With this kind of intelligence, we can endure anything. But more important, as we establish patience, we cultivate merit in this life and the next.

It's good to be a little afraid of aggression. Many think that
being motivated by fear is not good. But we all get insurance,
and we pay our premiums! If we were not afraid of tickets or
getting in an accident, we might go through red lights. But due
to our fear, we restrain ourselves. Studying other realms as described in the Buddhist scriptures informs us of the future consequences of our actions. For example, those who have a
propensity for killing and harming others experience a paranoid hellish existence. However, we don't need to go to such
extremes to observe the cause and effect of aggression. We see
it in ourselves, those around us, and even in movies and televi-
sion. Sometimes it helps to have something visual to relate to. I
have a friend whose son was stealing, so she sent him to a
prison in order that he could see what his options were. He
saw that prison was not just a place where inmates relaxed in

cells and watched TV. It put everything in perspective for him right away.

I read an inspiring story about a man in Tibet who had all the markings and characteristics of a demon. In fact, Padmasambhava, the Indian Mahasiddha who brought Buddhism to Tibet, predicted this man's coming in the Buddhist scriptures. This man knew about this prediction and recognized in himself his affinity for war and violence and all the signs described in the text. He recognized that his own weaknesses could harm both himself and others. So he sought out the great fourteenth-century meditation master and scholar, Kunkhyen Longchenpa. How unusual this is! Generally people don't want to identify themselves as demons! This is very touching, I think. It demonstrates how recognizing the qualities of aggression can turn our minds in the direction of peace. This is why in Alcoholics Anonymous people say, "I'm an alcoholic." People need to acknowledge that they need help, without feeling bad, and then seek an antidote.

SIMMERING PRACTICE

Once we have identified our aggressive tendencies, we can apply the principles of nonviolence. We will need to make a firm decision to *not* feed our aggression. If we were to go on a diet to slim down, for instance, we would need to refrain from old patterns of eating that don't support weight loss. Of course we would be able to eat—but no brownies! We would need to decide beforehand that brownies would not support our weight loss. Then, were the cravings to eat brownies to arise, we would need to practice abstinence—we would refrain from eating that brownie! It may seem natural to just go ahead and eat one, because that's our habit, and it might seem artificial to refrain. But our wisdom tells us that "the no-brownie way" provides the only path to weight loss. If we were to stick with this wisdom, we would have to simmer in the discomfort of not having our brownie. We would have to starve our brownie-eating tendency . . . and maybe go get a carrot stick instead. But in the end we would feel lighter and more confident about having moved forward with our aspirations.

Similarly, when we decide to practice nonviolence, we make a deliberate choice to simmer with our aggression. Simmering doesn't mean you boil in your aggression like a piece of meat cooking in a soup. It means you refuse to give in to anger because you know the result of aggression and you want to experience the confidence that comes from patience. So you summon up all your strength and let yourself feel how strong the tendency is, without rejecting it or giving in to it. In other words, simmering wears out the tendency to react habitually. Athletes do this in their own way. They love the pain of burning muscles when they exercise. They appreciate that kind of burning sensation because they know it makes them stronger and builds endurance.

Through the nonviolent practice of simmering, we can work to change our basic reactions to the world around us, and this has a positive effect on others. Then we can feel good and safe in the world of unpredictability, and we will not feel so intimidated by various states of mind, such as anger. In fact, when we simmer with our aggression, we not only burn the seeds or latent tendencies that give rise to further aggression, we also make good use of those seeds as an opportunity to cultivate patience. We might begin to question the nature of anger: What is anger, really, when we don't react to it? You might be surprised to find it isn't as substantial as you thought.

Many people consider reaching the peak of Mount Everest

a great accomplishment. But imagine accomplishing the practice of nonviolence. Through simmering in the raw discomfort of our tendencies, we can gain victory over our aggression and experience the confidence and well-being that come from patience. When you climb Mount Everest (and this is no insult to climbers), you still have to climb back down, but, accomplishing the practice of nonviolence, we just keep moving forward, building our confidence and sense of freedom. We move from one good place to an even better place. Because of the peace that comes from nonviolence and the pain that we experience from aggression, Shantideva, the eighth-century Indian master and author of the *Way of the Bodhisattva*, says that patience is the noblest austerity.

Most of us know at least one person who is really patient. Patient people seem to have a jovial mind, a mind that is happy at the root. Some people seem naturally patient, and we marvel at how lucky they are. But in most cases, a patient, jovial mind needs to be cultivated through the practice of tolerance and nonviolence. So much of this has to do with not just calming irritations but with how we shape our minds—how we replace aggression with patience. It requires a sense of broad-mindedness that comes from seeing the effects of aggression and, conversely, the effects of patience. This takes some contemplation. Someone told me recently that through simply contemplating the ways in which she feeds her mental unrest, she had the first good night's sleep she had had in a long time. That is what we all want, isn't it? A good night's sleep: a mind that is not reactive, a restful mind, a mind free from struggle.

4

Invisible Strings

A Case against Attachment

Attachment captures our peace of mind and holds it hostage. We become agitated, restless, and fixated like a dog when it sees a piece of meat—its mind can't settle, there's too much craving. It paces back and forth unable to focus on anything else. In Tibetan there is a term, *she cha sem lu*, that means that the mind is not where the body is. Our body wanders around like a ghost while the mind is somewhere else—obsessing on something—half present. Meanwhile, an invisible string connects us to this object, which continually tugs at our heart.

It often happens that when a mother leaves her baby at home, no matter where she goes, her mind is tied to the baby. She feels this pull whenever she thinks of him. The mother's mind is with the child, full of worries, while her body wanders around the store buying the milk . . . the eggs . . . the broccoli. The invisible string makes the mother vulnerable to many anxieties and irrational concerns. This is a common experience for mothers. It's not a bad thing. We may even consider it a noble thing. At the same time, there is suffering involved.

Likewise, our minds are tied to things. We go to Paris and put our large diamond in the hotel safe. Meanwhile, wandering through the streets of Paris, we walk past the Louvre and the Eiffel Tower; we come across an outdoor market where they sell local wine, cheese, and flowers; we walk down the Champs Élysées, but we don't notice any of it because we can't stop wondering, "Is my diamond safe? What if someone steals it? How can I be sure?" When we return home, everyone asks, "How was Paris?" We can't remember.

We have to wonder about our relationship to things, these things that supposedly bring us so much pleasure. On one hand, we chase after and relish them. On the other, they seem to function as a source of deep, deep dissatisfaction.

IMPOSSIBLE DEMANDS

A mind driven by craving and attachment is full of impossible demands. It expects continuous pleasure from what it believes to be its true sources of happiness: people, places, ideas, and things. We want to make them part of us, part of our lives. We don't want to depart from the many pleasures they bring us: the tastes, the sounds, the smells, and all the extraordinary sights!

Initially our fascination with these objects has a kind of dreamy allure full of fantasy and excitement . . . but then what happens? All of a sudden, when we have no contact with the desired object or the object doesn't perform as we expect, insecurities and anxieties begin to arise. The pleasure and happiness we had envisioned is nowhere in sight. In fact, we experience the complete opposite! We can't seem to acquire what we want. We can't hold on to what we have; things don't seem as attractive as they used to be. Yet strangely, we can't let go.

The mind stubbornly holds on, like an obedient slave that does as commanded, never engaging its intelligence or claiming its own strength. It cannot assert the right understanding or knowledge. It has lost possession of its contentment, integrity, and ability to self-reflect. Attachment has drugged the mind, reducing its potential to a bare minimum. It has dragged us by the hair into a dark alley and robbed us of all of our positive qualities, qualities we could use just now!

THE MYTH OF ROMANCE

The myth of romance takes hold of us at a young age. At the end of junior high school, we start to feel the pressure to be in love. At some point we like someone. When they enter the classroom, we flush and blush. Prior to this we were calm and composed, but, as soon as we decided we liked them, we started to get excited and awkward in their presence. Through mutual friends, we arrange for them to like us back. We convince our friends to give us a good "write-up" by treating them to movies and milk shakes. After they help us make it known to this person how we feel, we begin to send gifts—first indirectly. Later, we arrange to meet so we can openly confess how many months or days we have liked them. In severe cases, we might have to take a risk—like in *Romeo and Juliet*—sneaking across enemy lines to have a glimpse of our beloved. There is so much agony and so much willingness to go through hardships to sooth that agony!

If, by chance, this person is not that interested in being lured into our net, we have to be inventive, but not in an obvious way so that they get turned off (as opposed to turned on!). So we put a lot of resources into the task and maybe take some risks, for example, drinking a lot in order to impress and so forth. It all happens because, in that moment, the mind is really excited and getting closer to fulfillment, which may be just a private moment with a little physical contact.

If we are lucky, we capture the object of desire and make him or her "our own." Yet we soon find out that relationships are not so simple. People are complicated, and we have to take the whole package. We start to see many things that we hoped we would never see! All we wanted was to have someone sweet to cozy up with, to talk to, to have fun with and play with, to distract ourselves with so we don't have to feel lonely! But, instead of cozy, we get cold and brusque. Instead of fun and play, we receive thorny treatment. Instead of sweet, we get bitter and sour. Sure, the loneliness is gone, but now there are dynamics and we have to watch our beloved's moon-like face turn red, green, and black . . . the whole emotional gamut! It's almost a given that we will get bitten by our own hopes in some way!

This is not to say that we can't find pleasure in samsara. Sure we can! Temporal pleasure is samsara's dangling carrot. But lasting happiness? This is samsara's impossible promise. In time, life inevitably makes clear to us the discrepancies between our fantasies and how things really are, without our even trying to understand. It isn't some sort of evil master plan; it's just how things work.

PLEASURE OR PAIN?

The mind captivated by a state of craving has no clue as to what pain and pleasure really are. When we hanker after objects, do we experience peace and bliss? Are we in control? Do we feel at ease? Or do we feel restless? Stressed and worried? Insecure and desperate? The slippery thing about attachment is that, in our bewilderment, we can't tell the difference between pleasure and pain, love and desire, happiness and sorrow. The craving mind can mistake anything for pleasure—even pain! It's like an addiction.

When someone continues to ingest a substance that deteriorates his or her physical and mental well-being, despite the so-called pleasure it brings, we call it an addiction. If you know someone who has an addiction, you can see that addicts don't actually experience that much pleasure. They always seem restless and distracted—searching for a fix. There may be a moment's peace when they satisfy their yearning, but they spend most of their time hoping for satisfaction.

The driving force behind this hope is the fear of pain and discontentment. The fear of pain and discontentment generates hope, which, in turn, produces attachment. Attachment makes us vulnerable; it makes us dependent upon objects as a source of happiness. Without identifying the true causes of happiness and suffering, pleasure and pain, we swing back and forth between expecting objects to fulfill us and then blaming them for luring us in and making us unhappy. It's like eating sugar and crashing, and eating more sugar and crashing again—yum . . . yuck . . . yum . . . yuck. So how do we differ from an addict? If objects were a genuine source of happiness, we would be happy all the time, seeing as how there are so many desirable objects around us.

RENUNCIATION

We don't like to think about renunciation because it means we may have to give something up! We assume that it means rejecting all the pleasures of the world. But genuine renunciation doesn't come from rejection or avoidance; it comes from letting go of grasping and attachment.

When we begin to confront attachment, it's like having to open the door and search through our dark messy closet because there's something in there that stinks. We don't want to face it, even if we don't know what that something is. So we keep putting it off, but that rotting "thing" stays with us—we can't really dismiss it. If we could just put on some rubber gloves, get a flashlight and a plastic bag, go in there, see what it is, and remove it, it would be a big relief. If something in our lives causes us pain—if it doesn't serve us and is not essential to our well-being—why hold on?

When we can identify and let go of grasping, objects won't have the same power over us. They won't seduce us, tantalize us, or disturb us as they did before. So it is not necessary for us to rid ourselves of all of our belongings, cut off our relations, and resign ourselves to a life of austerity and gloominess. No one would suggest that because a mother has attachment for her child, she should simply do away with the child! No one ever says, "Wealth is bad; relations are bad! Get rid of those un-wholesome things!" Certainly there is no aggression like this in the buddhadharma!

At the same time, we need to see how our grasping to objects affects our mind and complicates our lives. Sometimes it is helpful to renounce the object as well as the grasping. For instance, it would obviously benefit an addict to give up drugs. And some people, like monks and nuns, choose to live a simple life in order to support their spiritual practice. Gathering, protecting, and increasing wealth can distract us for an entire lifetime. As Patrul Rinpoche says, "If you have a horse, you will have a horse's worth of trouble. If you have a bag of tea, you will have a bag of tea's worth of trouble." This speaks of the downside of samsara.

Everything in samsara has a downside. Some people really understand this. Once, when I went to Tibet, I brought a uniquely beautiful and rare statue with me. An old monk from my monastery was admiring it, and I felt inspired to offer it to him. When I did, he jumped back—literally three feet! He started politely refusing and gesturing: "No, no, no!" He could appreciate the attributes of the statue; he could rejoice that I had it, but in terms of keeping it, he just didn't want the trouble that he saw came with owning it.

We don't have to do away with everything we own, but maybe we could give up some investment in what we have. However we approach it, the point is to develop a little renunciation: to see how samsara works and how not to be lost in it forever. We need to let the suffering of attachment touch us, rather than getting carried away by its desires. In this way, the wisdom that understands the suffering of attachment can guide us in the right direction.

A LIFE WITHOUT ATTACHMENT

Some people might think that, without attachment, life would lose its juice. We are so habituated to the usual ups and downs, worries, stresses, and anxieties that we worry that if these go missing, so would all the love, care, enjoyment, and passions we experience. From this standpoint, life without conflicting emotions surging and churning all the time may seem a bit alien. But the boredom we fear is really just a state of unfulfilled desires, the flip side of the excitement and entertainment we habitually seek. It's still wholly within the realm of attachment's focus on getting or not getting, possessing or not possessing, keeping or not keeping, increasing or not increasing. Is there any true enjoyment in this?

Imagine craving absolutely nothing from the world. Imagine cutting the invisible strings that so painfully bind us: what would that be like? Imagine the freedoms that come from the ability to enjoy things without having to acquire them, own them, possess them. Try to envision a relationship based on acceptance and genuine care rather than expectation. Imagine feeling completely satisfied and content with your life just as it is. Who wouldn't want this? This is the enjoyment of nonattachment.

Seed of Contentment

The phenomenal world is much more fascinating and juicy when we stop grasping . . . wanting . . . craving. This is because the mind is present, the senses wide open, and the conceptual mind relaxed. We make tremendous space in our mind when we let go of this "can't live without it" desperation. And, when we discover the richness and contentment within our own mind, we find an answer to our lifelong question, "Where do I find satisfaction and contentment?"

There is a story of a destitute beggar who had an experience of freedom from his own desperation. He lived in India during the time of the Buddha. The Buddha saw him in the street and could see that he had been reborn in a deprived state of poverty five hundred times over. The Buddha told this man that he would give him a bag of gold if he could say, "I don't want it; I don't need it," three times. The beggar—so bereft of merit—had difficulty forcing out the words. But with the encouragement of the Buddha's attendant Ananda, he finally choked them out, "I don't want it; I don't need it." It was excruciatingly difficult. But he did it and received the bag of coins. This was the Buddha's kind ploy to help the beggar cultivate a seed of contentment and positivity in his own mind.

I have always found this story particularly touching. So one year when I went to India to make offerings, I decided to try it myself. I had a bag of coins and I came across a beggar in Bodh

Gaya, just like the one in the story. I told him I would offer him the bag of coins if only he would say, "I don't want it; I don't need it," three times. It was painful to watch him so conflicted and unable to respond. I thought he would miss the opportunity entirely. After a while, some Indian boys gathered around and shopkeepers came out of their shops. I knew many of them, and so they trusted me and began encouraging him. Soon they all cheered together, "Just say it! Say it!" People walking by joined in. Finally, at some point, he did it. And each time he repeated the words, I could literally see his whole presence and demeanor shift from a state of impoverishment to a state of recognition—a recognition of some inner strength and richness, or merit, that seemed to emerge from deep within. In the end, he accepted the coins in a dignified and noble way.

5

Entering the Circle of Dogs

A Case against Arrogance

Arrogance comes from the belief that we possess special attributes and that these attributes make us extraordinary in some way. We may feel proud of our attractive physical appearance, the sharpness of our intellect, or a position of power we hold. We may possess something unique—a great deal of wealth—that stands us apart from others. Or we may have a lot of charisma or a cool demeanor that projects an outward confidence, so that while others neurotically stumble around, we are able to hold it all together. We stand at the back of the room looking at the whole scenario thinking, "Just look at them!" This makes us feel special.

Certainly, these attributes can have their own worldly significance, and we can enjoy and appreciate them. But when we give them a special significance simply due to our ownership of them, we fall under the influence of our own conceit. We feel that they completely represent who we are and what we deserve, and we start to feel there is no one like us—that we are peerless.

Being peerless has its problems. We cannot maintain our high status on our own; we need others to agree. It takes a lot of affirmation to consistently be the best, and we never know how others will respond. This brings up a lot of insecurities for us: "Is

39

what I cherish really so worthy? What will others think? Do I really measure up? What if so-and-so doesn't think so!"

Even as our show gets stronger and more seamless on the outside and we feel kind of high, inside we get weaker and less sure that our attributes are as worthy as we initially imagined. Arrogance requires us to keep up false appearances, and with all the insecurities that we harbor underneath, this takes a lot of discipline and determination. All the qualities that we cherish just become something to manage—a self-imposed burden. Sometimes they provide us with a fragile sense of self-confidence. Other times we feel apologetic or self-conscious of them, wishing we didn't possess them at all. If someone compliments us, rather than simply saying thank you, we try to deflect it by putting ourselves down. Of course this only draws more attention to us and is entirely self-focused.

This may all seem pretty gross. We might think, "None of this sounds like me!" But, as long as we have a sense of "me," we will definitely find ourselves searching for some identity or another, for something to make "me" *me,* something to make "mine" *mine.* We may just want to be liked and can't understand why someone won't respond: "Don't they notice how likable, how enjoyable, how interesting I am?" Or, sometimes, we might try to promote ourselves through broadcasting our views. When others disagree or when they simply try to contribute to the conversation, we stop listening, because we think we know everything already. Sometimes we may ask one token question just to show that we're listening, although we already think we know the answer. There's a lot of output but not much coming in, because who needs to listen when we're already perfect? You may think that you possess none of these tendencies. If so, you might just want to take another look.

FALLING DOWN

According to Buddhist cosmology, pride is related to the worldly god realms. The gods have pride in their attributes of beauty and wealth. Because they find so much satisfaction in their existence, they have little renunciation or even awareness of suffering. They live long lives full of sensory enjoyments and leisure. But at the end of their lives, their beauty starts to fade and the flower garlands that adorn their bodies begin to rot. None of their beloved friends will come near them because it reminds them of their own mortality. After death, rejected and despondent, they immediately fall into the lower realms.

Arrogant mind is terrified of loss, terrified of falling down and being exposed as "ordinary." Someone may discover that we are not actually as special, unique, magnificent, incredible, intelligent, or "deep" as we let on. We may fall from supermodel stardom, the top of the heap, from the status of being the most handsome and powerful. Someone may catch a glimpse of our neurotic mind and learn that we may not actually be enlightened after all. Even if we believe we have indisputable intelligence, creativity, or beauty, someone else's contrary opinion can knock us right off our pedestal.

When we are the king or queen of beauty, good ideas, intelligence, or even "spirituality," we can't bear the thought of anyone becoming equal to us or, even worse, stealing our crown! Of course, the minute we think like this, all the good qualities drain out of our mind. Any kind of admiration or appreciation for anything other than "me" and "mine" dissolves. Anything in the world worthy of honor we are unable to honor. Anything worthy of respect we are unable to respect. We find ourselves denigrating everything, defiling everything, critically judging everything, and making everything that is good for others insignificant.

In this way, arrogance isolates. When we see others as a threat, we stop reaching out and we can't ask for help because it makes us look weak. We are unable to mix with people in a decent way, in a common or ordinary way. We simply don't want to walk on the same ground as others.

A QUESTION OF IDENTITY

The arrogant mind never stops searching for identity, and this identity always defines itself through attributes: "the beautiful one," "the smart one," "the creative one," "the successful one." Sometimes we take this further by creating a more elaborate persona: "the rebel," "the maverick," "the suffering artist," "the fearless leader." We can hold on to these labels on a "good" day. But when we feel insecure about our attributes, or our lack thereof, we start to wonder how to define ourselves; we wonder who it is we really are. Regardless of whether we're having a good day or a low–self-esteem day, the point is, we haven't found a way to relax, to be natural, unself-conscious. We don't know how to take our seat in ordinariness and feel comfortable in our own skin. We're always searching for something to *be*. It's like having an ongoing identity crises.

Many people say that the remedy for the search for identity comes through developing a healthy ego—a strong sense of self—but feeling that we don't know who we are or why we exist does not indicate a lack of ego at all. In fact, in our search for identity, ego is the principle contributor to our confusion, offering only two questionable options: inflation or deflation. When we are deflated, it is simply arrogant mind in a state of not having. When we are inflated, it's nothing more significant than arrogant mind fattening up the minute it gets a chance. Both are due to the arrogant mind's unwillingness to be ordinary and its inability to appreciate in a successful way the attributes we do possess.

The truth is that our attributes are not possessable. Everything in our lives arises from causes and conditions, and in time, causes and conditions will take them away. No one is truly self-made from the start. So many factors contribute to who we are—we are not a closed system. We cannot hold a position without the support of others. All of the knowledge we have absorbed has come from our parents, our teachers, and the environment we grew up in. If we are beautiful, we necessarily have to attribute our beauty to our parents (or maybe our surgeon)—it is not self-created. We may even be the leaders of the free world, but we were elected. How can we honestly lay claim to any of these positions? We may know a lot about basket weaving, religion, fashion design, music, or exporting foreign goods, but all of these attributes—whether temporal or spiritual—are provided to us through the hard work of others. So, rather than taking all the credit and feeling cocky because we have so much to offer with our incredible creativity, we should see ourselves as the recipients of others' kindness. The minute we try to own our attributes and identify with them, they turn around and bite us where it counts. I don't think we can really appreciate our attributes without understanding this point.

HUMILITY AND APPRECIATION

When we recognize the source of our attributes, they become less personal and we can enjoy them. Rather than defining who we are, they can serve the function of enriching our lives as well as others'. Appreciation unleashes all the inherent positive qualities of mind. Appreciating others has a unifying effect and brings us out of our isolation. When we appreciate others' significant qualities with a clear mind, it is as if we have lassoed these qualities with our recognition and pulled them closer to us so that they enrich our own mind as well. This kind of appreciation is associated with humility. Humility is an attractive quality, one universally cherished. It affects our mind, our speech, and it beautifies our physical presence, too.

In the old days, someone might have proclaimed, "I'm so-and-so from such and such a place, from the such and such clan!" Nowadays, no one cares. Modern society puts much more emphasis on credentials and encourages us to accumulate them. On a more fundamental level, people naturally discriminate between the self-conscious crassness of arrogance and the grace of humility and ordinariness. When people try to sell themselves, no matter how attractive they may be, our natural response is to walk away. Human intelligence understands this well.

So we need to genuinely recognize the contributions of others in our lives, not by simply thinking, "Oh yes, these people have contributed, but it is *I* who have pulled it all together," or, "*I* am really the one who has done this amazing thing." Genuine appreciation is not Hollywood-style appreciation. It's not like standing up at the Academy Awards and saying, "I'd like to thank my director, my producer, and . . . I love you, Mom!" but secretly thinking, "Wow, me! I'm the star!" Appreciation has to be genuine, from within.

People with appreciation and humility are often the most respected members of society. We sometimes see people who started from scratch; maybe all they owned was a small teashop. If they ran their business based on ethical principles, if they stayed decent and humble, then over time, even having succeeded in business, they remain the same. These people are valued by society. Someone will say, "Oh, he's exactly the same now as when he owned that modest teashop, remember?" This statement expresses an appreciation of that person's humility.

Entering the Circle of Dogs

rul Rinpoche says, "The low seat is the high seat, the noble seat." Why is this? The answer: because there is nowhere to fall. The low seat is the noble seat because it grounds us in ordinariness and humility. It protects us from our own insecurities and comparing mind. Of course, in society at times, we may need to take a position of authority or leadership, we may need to sit at the head of the table or even on a throne, but as long as we remain humble we can't fail.

The Kadampas* taught, "Leave the human circle, and enter the circle of dogs. Then you will obtain the divine state." This means that when we live amongst humans, we have to operate from human values. This often entails trying to become as unique and special as possible. We have to accumulate the credentials valued in the human world and so are bound to compare ourselves with others and use them as a barometer for our successes and failures.

But if we leave the league of humans and enter the realm of dogs—nonsignificants—we enter the divine state free of pride and comparing. We enter the place from which there is nowhere to fall—the lowest seat. It is a humble place to take a seat. It is a place where all negative emotions subside. It is a place of humility and ordinariness. We can rest like an old dog with no need for confirmation and no fear of opposition. All is like space.

---

*The tradition of study and practice taught by the Indian master Atisha (982–1054).

6

Connecting Seed and Fruit

A Case against Stupidity

All beings, from the smallest insect to the most learned scholar, strive for happiness and freedom from suffering. Unfortunately, the ways in which we try to achieve happiness do not always accord with this aspiration. When we don't know how to bring our actions together with our intentions, there must be some sort of confusion or bewilderment in our minds, some sort of stupidity.

While *ignorance* is simply the state of not knowing, *stupidity* is the dull state of mind that allows us to repeat the same thing over and over again despite its negative consequences. Stupidity shares a partnership with the other disturbing emotions, for instance, in the way we get burnt again and again by our own aggression or the way, when coupled with attachment, stupidity supports our addictions. The persistent indifference and murkiness of stupidity allow us to continually re-create our mistakes, even if they make us sick.

Stupidity is a mind on cruise control. A mind enveloped in stupidity is completely oblivious to the laws of cause and effect, seed and fruit. It doesn't connect happiness with the causes of happiness or suffering with the causes of suffering. It just fills up its gas tank and heads out, moving along with a complete lack of inquisitiveness.

Of course, we usually have a clear idea of how we'd like our lives to be. If asked, "Would you rather be happy or rich?" or "Would you rather be happy or powerful?" most anyone would choose happiness. No one would say, "I couldn't care less about being happy. I just want money. I would rather be miserable and rich." Yet we entirely structure our lives—all our effort, energy, and resources—around worldly attainments, such as wealth and power. And we don't often question whether or not this fulfills our intention for happiness, because we are consumed by our immediate needs—constantly engaging in the upkeep of our own created web of pain. The dismissive or passive quality of stupidity can prevent us from even noticing that we are just plodding along in life, not really enjoying or finding any meaning in it. Having resigned ourselves to this state, we develop some "resilience" that enables us to endure the suffering and meaninglessness of life . . . that is, until that one day when our skull hits the ground.

Stupidity becomes a standard for us in this way. Whether we experience the passivity of stupidity or, on the other hand, find ourselves stubbornly fixed in our views, completely "not open for negotiation," the suffering of stupidity is there in all of us. It is everywhere. Wherever we look, there it is in everyone's life. This is something very large. We're not talking about two or three people. We're not talking about one hundred or even one million. We're talking about billions of people suffering because their actions don't meet their intention for happiness.

THE PAIN OF BEING DUMBFOUNDED

Most animals can't discern, beyond their programmed instincts to survive, the relationship between causes and results. They respond to habitual conditioning or punishment and reward, but the ability to self-reflect does not generally exist for them. Sometimes we hear incredible stories about animals where they express an amazing amount of compassion and intelligence. But in general, their focus moves from one tuft of grass to the next. In a blizzard, cows often just stand there and freeze because they don't have the capacity to strategize. Entire herds of animals have been known to jump off cliffs when chased. Understand that this is not to embarrass or put down animals, it just speaks of the pain of stupidity they experience.

Unlike animals, human beings have an acute ability to reason and discern between right and wrong, and we function in the world of cause and effect all the time—we pay our bills, hold a job, and find ways to feed and clothe ourselves. In school we may collect a lot of information about the world and how to live effectively in it. Yet we often still find ourselves disengaged from our own clarity, moving along without thinking, in ways that are not much different from animals.

Our intelligence may be exceptionally sharp, but we can still live out an entire lifetime without solving the fundamental question of happiness. Subconsciously we know that there must be something we can do, and we want to do whatever that is, but we can't access the knowledge. So a feeling of paralyzing inferiority invades our minds. Getting frozen in the state of being dumbfounded is a big source of suffering for us because we don't find much contentment in life when our actions don't meet our intentions.

When we simply resign ourselves to circumstances in this way, we start to relate to our lives with a kind of casualness or cool indifference. Unlike other emotions that are hard to ignore—such as aggression—stupidity can be inconspicuous in a way that allows us to just blank out. We may think that the indifference of stupidity is a neutral experience, but that isn't true. Stupidity causes harm because we continue in an unintended direction, a direction that, in the deepest sense, we don't want to go in.

People can call us all sorts of names, but when somebody calls us stupid, it cuts to the bone. It makes us feel disrespected as human beings. This is because stupidity is the most undermining form of suffering—the lowest of the low.

The Sting of Suffering

Sometimes we need dramatic occurrences to wake us up from our stupor so that we can see what's at stake and can recognize how fleeting life really is. We often hear stories of people who are just going about their daily lives until suddenly they find out that they have cancer. This is a life-changing, awakening experience for some. It is not uncommon to hear people say that cancer, or some other calamity, has changed their lives, that it has put things into perspective, straightened out their priorities—in other words, it stops them in their tracks and wakes them up. It's like having been caught up in a daydream and suddenly getting startled by a loud noise or stung by a bee. Immediately, all our senses open up, and we begin to inquire about what is going on around us.

Stupidity always has an undercurrent of pain running through it, which is lucky because we need to be able to feel the pain of our situation. Pain activates the intelligence that otherwise lies dormant in the stupid state of mind. When we experience pain, it can awaken us and point us in the right direction. When we look at the life of the Buddha, we can see that the very pain we all confront—the suffering of change, uncertainty, and death—served as the very means for his awakening. Unable to dismiss pain, he kept his eyes open and didn't shrink away from the wakefulness and truthfulness of it. Ultimately, pain served as the cause for his enlightenment. This is why we contemplate suffering—to wake up from our stupor and see what is at stake.

This kind of wake-up call doesn't necessarily mean we know exactly what to do in each and every situation or that we can see what lies ahead. But at least, whatever happens, the mind is present to engage it. "Not knowing" can be an open, inquisitive, and humble state of mind, full of possibilities—there's a lot to explore. With inquisitiveness, we engage our intelligence, educate ourselves, and move forward in our lives in a way that satisfies our deeper needs. This is the knowledge that comes through hearing the truth. To do this, we first have to feel the pain of our situation—the antidote is right there, just beneath the surface.

Part Two

WORKING
WITH OTHERS

7

The *Lenchak* Dynamic

Not a Healthy Kind of Love

We all have some rough relationships in our lives that seem held together by the stickiness of attachment and expectation. It is true that we have love and care for these people, but, at the same time, it's not so clean; there's plenty of complexity. Inside, we feel an emotional tug when we see or think of them. This is often exaggerated with the people we are close to and with whom we share a strong dynamic, such as our parents, children, close friends, or spouse—all relationships where a lot of expectations tend to arise. There are many unspoken demands. In the midst of our romance, marriage, or parenting, we find ourselves responsible for someone else's loneliness and their emotional or physical pain.

There is a Tibetan term that describes this kind of dynamic, *lenchak*, commonly translated as "karmic debt." *Len* literally means "time" or "occurrence," while *chak* refers to "attachment," "attraction," or the notion of a karmic pull toward someone, usually in an unhealthy way. So lenchak could be understood as the residue that revisits us from the dynamic of a relationship from a past life, a dynamic now strengthened by reoccurring habitual responses. Lenchak is most often used to explain or describe why a particular relationship is how it is.

In the Buddhist texts, it says that in certain hell realms beings experience the negative results of past unwholesome relationships. They hear their name being called out and experience a pull toward the voice of the person they once knew. They travel toward that voice but end up encountering horrendous creatures and experiencing intense physical and mental anguish. This is interesting because, with those with whom we have lenchak, we feel an immediate pull beyond our control or sense of resistance. Our name is called, and we jump to at once to serve them. This is not a conscious decision—not a joyous decision—but more like being propelled by a strong wind. Our reaction—whether with anger, jealousy, attachment, or what have you—only serves to reinforce the dynamic. People have done many things "in the name of love." But if this is love, it's not a healthy kind of love.

THE SEAL AND THE OWL

In Tibet they say there is a lake where, during a particular full moon each year, the seal-like creatures who live there gather fish in their mouths and offer them up to hordes of owls who hover in the trees above, waiting to eat. There is no apparent reason for the seals to offer the fish other than the fact that the owls seem to expect it. As the story goes, the seals gain nothing from offering the fish, and the owls are never satisfied. So, they say, since there is no obvious reason for this dynamic to be as it is, "it must be lenchak."

The lenchak dynamic has two sides: the seal side and the owl side. If we are the seal, we feel an unspoken emotional responsibility for someone else's mind and well-being. We feel pulled toward this person as if they had a claim on us. It's a strong visceral experience, and we have a physical reaction to it:

The phone rings and we check our caller-ID—it's "the owl." We *should* pick it up, but we are overcome by a strong wave of anxiety and repulsion, as if we are being attacked by our own nervous system. We brace ourselves for a problem or a strong emotional download. As much as we want to detach ourselves from this person, we can't break loose; it's as if they have captured us, and there's no escape—checkmate! Of course, this is not the case. In truth we are held hostage by our own attachment, guilt, and inability to resist the pain that comes from feeling unreasonably responsible for them. On one hand, we can't bare watching the owl struggle. On the other hand, we can't let go. This dynamic brings us down; it makes us lose our luster as human beings.

Meanwhile, the owl is never satisfied, no matter how many fish the seal tries to feed it. Of course, when caught in the owl syndrome we don't see it in this way. We feel neglected, isolated, and weak. The reason for this is that we are depending on someone else in hopes that they will manage our fears. We have so many unspoken demands, although we often express these demands in a meek and needy way. The owl syndrome reduces us to a childlike state. We begin to question whether or not we can do things on our own, and we lose confidence in our ability to face our own mind and emotions. Interestingly, the owl—so frail, needy, and insecure—is not necessarily as feeble as it seems to be. In fact, the owl has the upper hand. It's a little manipulative if you want to know the truth. The owl just doesn't want to clean up its own mess. This is a privileged attitude. If the owl couldn't afford to be weak—if it didn't have the seal—it would naturally rise to its own challenges.

The irony of this dynamic is that, in most cases, the more fish the seal offers the owl, the more resentful, demanding, and dissatisfied the owl gets. For both the seal and owl, this kind of dependence and expectation gives way to a lot of ugliness. At work we may have to hold our tongues and swallow what our boss has to say, but there is no holding back with our loved ones. We let our guard down and allow ourselves to get ugly, spreading our web of ego anxieties all over the place. It's true; the seal may temporarily pacify the owl, but no mutual respect arises from this kind of arrangement. And in truth, isn't it respect that we want most of all? Everyone wants love and care, but, more than these, human beings want respect for who they are. Even an enemy can respect another enemy. There is a sense of human dignity in this.

In this confusion of lenchak for love, we fear that without the lenchak dynamic our relationships will completely fall apart. What is there beyond all the obligations, all the "shoulds" and "shouldn'ts," and all the fantasies we try to live up to? The distinction between love and lenchak needs to be examined carefully. Love and care toward others warms the heart and makes us generous and giving. Feelings of love and care arise naturally; they are not the product of pressures and demands. Think about the attachment and pain of lenchak. Think of all the insecurities and resentment that come with it. Lenchak makes us feel like we are not up for our own life and its challenges or that we can't handle seeing others in pain. And yet, we don't trust that they can handle their own lives either!

RISING TO THE OCCASION

When it's time for a child to start walking, a mother needs to let her child walk. She needs to let the child lose his or her balance, fall down, and then find balance once again. Alone, the child needs to get up and stand on his or her own two feet. Although children need protection, we need to have confidence in their potential to flourish. We don't want to hold them captive by our

own fears and doubts—this creates the unhealthy dependence
we have been talking about. Letting children immerse themselves in a challenging situation or obstacle for a while gives the
child confidence. It gives the mother confidence too. It's one of
the early steps a mother takes in letting the child become a cit-
izen of the world.

When challenges or obstacles arise for us, we don't have to
get so intimidated; we can say, "Yes, it's an obstacle, but it is not
intrinsically bad; it's not going to destroy me." To create a relationship with the obstacle, learn about it, and finally overcome
the obstacle is going to be a helpful thing to do. It gives us a
chance to cultivate wisdom and skillful means. It gives us confidence. We cannot eliminate all of the challenges or obstacles
in life—our own or anyone else's. We can only learn to rise to
the occasion and face them. Shantideva suggests that we need
to cultivate a "Can do! Why not? No problem!" kind of attitude
toward our neuroses and obstacles in order to overcome them.
If we have no confidence, we'll already be defeated, like a dead
snake lying on the ground. Around a dead snake, even a sparrow
can act like a *garuda*!* In the same way, the smallest fear or neurosis will entirely overpower us.

The great deception of lenchak is that it doesn't even occur
to us that our suffering is our own. We automatically expect that
others should share in it or take it on themselves. In this way,
lenchak gets in the way of us owning up to the responsibility of
our lives. There are times when we try to pull others in for sym-
pathy. If asked, "How are you?" we will review our full history. It
starts off, "I'm OK, but . . ." We feel a need to share everything.
At the end of the conversation, others know all our troubles and

---

*An ancient mythological Indian bird, said to be able to travel from one end of the universe
to the other with a single movement of its wings. *Garudas* are also said to hatch from the
egg fully developed, and are thus used as a symbol for the awakened state of mind.

ailments. We just can't seem to go through the process on our own with our own strength.

But do we really need to be transparent as glass? Do others really want this kind of honesty? People often can't handle all the details and confusion in their own lives! It is safe to assume that they have emotional ups and downs and uncomfortable physical sensations like us. Furthermore, unless they are our doctor what can they actually do for us?

At the end of my mother's life, when she was quite sick, an old friend came to see her. When he asked how she was feeling, she said, "I'm fine." I later asked her why she said that, and she replied, "What else should I say?" When you ask accomplished teachers how they are, they always say, "Good, good, very good"—always good. Many people say that they feel dishonest saying they are good when in fact they have problems. But what we are talking about here is developing a fundamental sense of strength and well-being. Wouldn't it be better to associate our mind with that rather than with all the fleeting emotions and physical sensations we experience throughout the day? What is the point of being honest about something so fleeting and im- possible to pin down? If your well-being is so dependent upon your emotions and physical sensations, you will have little op- portunity to say, "I am well." So when people ask how you are, say, "Good!" You may need to pump yourself up a little bit in the beginning, but soon you will start to believe it yourself. You will begin to see that people feel more attracted to you. They won't feel that subtle tug when they see you coming. And they will be less hesitant to ask how you are!

THE PRACTICE OF GENTLE DISENGAGEMENT

When we are bound by the emotional needs of others, or simply afraid of our own, how can we entertain the idea of engaging a spiritual path? And when our relationships with others are so unclean and confused, how can we expect to extend kindness to others and work for their benefit? Lenchak goes against the most fundamental principles of spiritual practice. We are always seeking something from the outside and forgetting that our fundamental well-being and strength depend on how we relate to our own minds. Falling under the sway of the lenchak dynamic is like losing possession of our very lives. It's like letting others lead us around by the nose ring as if we were a buffalo or a cow. What could be more detrimental than losing our freedom in this way?

All the great practitioners know the consequences and pitfalls of lenchak and so fiercely guard their independence. They are savvy when it comes to working with others because they know that, whether it concerns their students, parents, family, or whoever, if they fell prey to the lenchak dynamic, it would eat up their time and their peace of mind too. Moreover, because it is a dynamic based on neurosis, lenchak leaves no supportive ground on which to serve others. In the end, they would find themselves leading an entirely different life from the spiritual life of practice they envisioned for themselves.

Knowing this, many yogis have steered clear of societal demands and led simple lives, traveling alone without the complications that come with having many sponsors and attendants. Patrul Rinpoche had a strong, uncompromising presence and was completely immune to any kind of deception or partiality. There are stories that when important dignitaries would come for an audience—some of them so proud it would have taken a bulldozer to get their heads down—they would shake like prayer flags in his presence. But don't think for a moment that Patrul Rinpoche, even though he was free of entanglements, had even a trace of indifference! He was known as a loyal and kind friend, a compassionate friend, who dedicated his life solely for the benefit of others. Because he was able to see the greater potential of the human mind's ability to awaken, he spent his entire life expounding the teachings with great care and tenderness. Through his wisdom and compassion, he was able to preserve his independence and serve others, perfecting his own mind through the jewel of *bodhichitta*.*

Wisdom and compassion are the two components of bodhichitta. When we begin to discover the mind's natural potential and strength, we are cultivating wisdom. This doesn't mean we become hard-hearted and indifferent. It doesn't mean we have to cut our family ties, quit our job, or live in a cave. It simply means we refuse to give in to lenchak because we see that it doesn't serve us and that it makes it impossible for us to serve others. We recognize lenchak, and we can "just say no!" We can see it as a form of civil disobedience—a nonviolent approach in which we refuse to succumb to our own and others' ignorance. When we can reclaim our nose ring, we are left with no real reason to resent others. With a mind free from lenchak, we have a lot of room to expand the heart through serving others. This is how wisdom can protect us, so that we can be soft and caring. This is the bodhisattva's way.

In the sutras it says that a bodhisattva is like an immaculate lotus that floats on muddy water. The lotus is a metaphor for the bodhisattva who engages the world of confusion in order to serve beings. But how is it that the bodhisattva stays afloat without sinking into the muddy water of confusion? It is due to the wisdom of knowing the mind—how it can serve us or how,

Bodhichitta means "enlightened heart." On the relative level, bodhichitta has two aspects: aspiration bodhichitta, which is the wish to attain enlightenment in order to bring all living beings to liberation; and engaged bodhichitta, which includes such practices as generosity and patience. On the absolute level, bodhichitta is insight into the nature of all phenomena.

if left unchecked, it can spin in the direction determined by confusion. This kind of clarity may seem a long way off for us, but it all begins with rising to the occasion of our lives and facing our minds. We need to think clearly about this. Since this is our life, we must find some determination to rise to it in a way that supports our aims. Once we taste the freedom that comes with independence, it gets easier. We realize how much we have lost by desperately holding on, and we know how much there is to gain through disengaging from confusion. We can do this while expanding our most precious qualities: our good heart and our compassion for others. Through our innate qualities of wisdom and compassion, we can burn the seeds of lenchak once and for all, ensuring benefit for both self and other. This knowledge has been of great personal value to me in my life as a teacher, householder, and friend. I hope that it serves you well, too.

8

Part of the Equation

No Room for Indifference

Our relationships with others extend far beyond the friends and relatives of this lifetime. Throughout our countless lives we have mingled with and bumped up against all kinds of beings in all manner of ways. We have touched them, cared for them, and nurtured them, but we have also milked them dry, eaten them, and stepped on them. We have offended and abused them both mentally and physically. Thinking only of ourselves, we have enjoyed great wealth at their expense and misused the power we were given. In doing so, we have influenced the course of their lives, and they have influenced ours. Most of these beings we don't even know and have never seen.

Relationships are central to human existence. We rely on others for the food we eat, the clothes we wear, and all the information and knowledge we gather throughout our lives. Think about the planting, harvesting, and transportation of food. Many small insects die in the process of cultivating the soil. Pesticides harm wildlife such as fish and birds. Farm workers labor in the hot sun for small wages. Meanwhile, the mind of a farmer is filled with anxiety: "Will the crops be good? Will the weather cooperate?" If we follow the news, we don't have to think hard about what goes into obtaining the fuel we use for

65

farming machinery and transportation. The food we eat literally depends upon the blood, sweat, and tears of others. As Patrul Rinpoche says, "All the factors we now see constituting happiness—food to eat, clothes to wear, and whatever goods and materials we can think of—are likewise produced through negative actions alone. . . . Everything that seems to represent happiness today is, in fact, suffering in the making."* In this way, we are all part of the equation of suffering.

We might try to turn a blind eye to the suffering of others and go about taking care of our basic needs, forgetting the whole idea of interdependence altogether. But is that even possible? And if it were, can you imagine leading a meaningful life just thinking about "me, myself, I"? We may try to lessen the negative impact we have on our environment. We may become a vegetarian or take the bus rather than relying on a car. We may start our own garden or diligently recycle all of our containers. No doubt, respecting the natural laws of interdependence creates harmony in the world and helps us see a bigger picture than we would if we were only thinking of our own needs. But no matter how hard we try, we will always depend on others and we will always have to accept the bittersweet quality that pervades all of our relationships. Simply through the process of being alive we accumulate debt, and there is no escaping it.

DEBT AND INDEBTEDNESS

How does debt play out in our lives? Debt forms the basis of our relationships with others, some of which have a history we can trace and some not. We run into someone in the street who pro-

*The Words of My Perfect Teacher, trans., Padmakara Translation Group (Boston: Shambhala Publications, 1998), p. 80.

vokes a sense of fear in us and steals our wallet. Then, out of the
blue, someone we've never met extends a great kindness. And,
as for our children and spouse, how or why did these particular
beings enter our lives in this intimate kind of way? Sometimes
our children have such distinctive predilections and personalities that it makes us wonder where they actually came from.
Some relationships are so volatile we seem to have little or no
control over them—as if the dynamic controlled everything.
Sometimes we come across people who seem unreasonably
needy and expectant of our care, beyond our ability to help, even
when we want to. And what about our enemies? We go to war
with those we've never met—who, in turn, want to bring us
down. What is the history we share with them? What is the
debt we owe them? And what is the debt they owe us?

"Debt" is a heavy word. It brings to mind burden and guilt,
credit-card bills and bank loans. No one ever wants to be in
debt. Debt is a condition we find ourselves in. However, if
someone were to save our life, for instance, our response would
be one of indebtedness and appreciation. Of course, we would
still encounter the weightiness of that debt, but most likely we
would take that on without hesitation and try to repay this person's kindness in any way possible. Indebtedness toward this
person would be a positive experience and bring out our most
positive qualities, as it often does when we feel appreciation for
our parents or anyone who has shown us care and has taken us
under their wing.

Indebtedness reminds us of our humanity. When we feel
indebted, we think about the way we use things, consume
things, and where they came from. We begin to notice the people we brush up against on the street each day: the lady at the
bank, the waitress who serves us coffee, the UPS man who de-
livers our parcels. We start to pay attention to the people on the

subway and the homeless living on the street. We start to think about the small everyday exchanges we have with others: How do they effect and shape our lives? These are not random happenings. They are fleeting expressions of our connectedness to others. When we have gratitude toward others, we feel touched by our relationship with beings living in this world of unpredictability and change. The fact that we accumulate debt by virtue of living in samsara is an unsolvable dilemma—something that can't be fixed. But our indebtedness toward others touches our heart and stirs our compassion, creating no room for indifference.

Putting Others in the Center

The Fundamental Principle

Our human search for happiness and freedom from suffering expresses itself in everything we do. We emerge from the womb with a primordial instinct to find comfort through suckling our mother's milk. Our instinct for fulfillment drives us—it is not something we need to cultivate. Throughout our countless lifetimes, we have searched for happiness and freedom from pain. We have always been sentient; therefore we have always had this longing. It lies at the very core of our being.

Animals long for happiness, too. We see it in their propensity to frolic. Play doesn't simply fulfill an evolutionary function; it is an expression of pleasure and joy. As human beings, we understand the joy and freedom that comes from play. We also witness animals' desire for freedom from suffering. Animals fight for survival: their lives consist of trying to protect themselves from predators; they move in herds, hide in their shells, or fly off when afraid. When kept in tight cages, mistreated, or about to be slaughtered, animals cry out in pain.

The natural principle that all beings long for happiness and freedom from suffering serves as the basis for generating compassion. The longing that we share with other beings makes empathy possible—it allows us to identify with their pain and their joy. According to the Buddhist view, this natural principle defines positive and negative actions by virtue of how they cause happiness and pain, rather than by morals based on ideas that are remote from our experience. The path of *bodhichitta*—the wish for others' temporal and ultimate happiness—rests upon this fundamental principle.

A CHANGE OF FOCUS

The longing for happiness and freedom from suffering ex-presses the great natural potential of mind, which can turn us toward our innate positivity and wisdom. Yet we may wonder why, if we have so much longing for happiness, joy is not a con-sistent experience. We may wonder why we feel like a victim of our own mind and emotions so much of the time. Why is it we are never able to completely fulfill or meet this longing, no mat-ter what we do?

This longing remains unfulfilled because we attempt to centralize it—to territorialize it and use it to serve only our-selves. Day in and day out we tend to the self. In countless ways we attempt to use the world to cherish and protect only our-selves: We want to be liked; we want to be loved, to feel cozy, admired, appreciated, embraced, cherished, stimulated, noticed, respected, saved, rescued. When we centralize our longing for happiness, everything that happens around us happens in rela-tion to *me*. If something good happens to someone else, it is al-ways in relation to *me*. If something bad happens to someone else, it always happens in relation to *me*. Even when we love someone, it is all in relation to *me*.

If happiness could be achieved through self-cherishing, we

would certainly be happy by now. But when everything is in reference to "me," we naturally become a victim of our own aggression, attachments, and fears. How can we succeed in living our lives according to our preferences in the face of the natural laws of change and unpredictability? Since we truly have so little control in this respect, the only logical result of focusing on "me" is to feel distraught, fearful, and anxious.

Happiness requires we change our focus. Changing focus doesn't mean we have to get rid of our mind; we don't need to change the basic makeup of the mind at all. We simply need to honor the fundamental principle by including others in our wish for happiness rather than focusing solely on ourselves. Self-care is always there. When we balance self-care with care for others, we reduce our fears and anxieties. Self-service is always there; all our wants and "unwants" are always there. Expanding our thinking to include others' wants and others' freedoms, we begin to move toward a happiness that is not reliant on the conditions and preferences of self-care.

When we put others in the center, tenderness wells up from within. We feel grateful to others—witnessing their suffering brings us out of the rotten cocoon we sleep in. It makes us a little bit fearless, a little bit accepting, a little bit willing to let go of the constricted sense of self we hold on to. This kind of empathy changes the whole atmosphere of mind. It is the purest form of happiness. The sutras ask, where do the buddhas come from? And the answer in the sutras is, they come from ego. What does this mean? This means that realization comes from our ability to expand our sense of self-care and longing for happiness to include others. This is the business of a bodhisattva.

DECENTRALIZING SELF

The idea of putting others in the center sounds good but, as a practice, may feel contrived. As much as we want to expand our heart to include others, we can't simply leap into a state of compassion and loving-kindness when, in our attempts at self-preservation, we recoil from the experience of our own pain. True happiness cannot be found through the avoidance of pain. We can't decentralize our longing for happiness when we desperately hold to our own well-being. The tendency to constrict the heart is driven by habit and motivated by fear. It is a deep-rooted and visceral experience. We can feel it in our bodies. It follows us like a shadow.

Shutting out suffering is an extremely dangerous non-dharmic act because through our aversion we exclude the full experience of mind. We deny impermanence and attempt to keep things in control; we ignore the truth. In short, we can't relax and let things be. In the act of abandoning the truth through rejection, we individuate ourselves from everything around us. In doing so, we don't allow ourselves a bigger, expanded experience that is inclusive of our world and the other beings in it.

Ironically, we shrink from a pain that doesn't actually exist. We speak about the *truth* of suffering only in that we experience it. But what is suffering really when we stop trying to push it away? This kind of questioning needs to be the theme of our lives. We need to take delight in working with our fears. We need to study them and ask ourselves, "What am I so afraid of? Why do I need to protect myself?" We may be afraid to shed our burden because we don't know what will happen. Suffering seems to define our lives. Can we imagine a life without it?

The purpose of all practices on the Buddhist path is to decentralize this notion of a solid, independent "self." This does not mean that we stop functioning as an individual, that we forget our name and wander about aimlessly like a zombie. It means we stop relating to everything in a way that aims only at preserving or cherishing ourselves. When we begin to question the autonomy of "me," the constricted self begins to disperse, which is another way of saying that our ignorance begins to dissolve and we move toward wisdom. Putting others in the center is a powerful method for decentralizing the self. When the self expands to include others, exclusivity is overwhelmed by compassion in the same way that darkness disperses in sunlight.

The practice of putting others in the center is not simply a crusade to do "good." It is a practice based on the understanding that our own happiness is inextricably linked with the happiness of others. We understand that the longing we all have for happiness and freedom from suffering can be a curse or a blessing depending solely on our focus.

10

Faith

Opening the Shutters

The mind has the ability to express itself in any way at all—
that's its nature. You can say this is both a blessing and a
curse. The beauty of it is that anything and everything is possible. The curse is that, if we surrender to our weaknesses, giving
into every thought and emotion, we will never be at ease. We
need to have confidence that there are things we can rely on to
support our well-being and anchor us to a sense of fundamental sanity. When everything falls away, when nothing seems to
make sense, we have to hang on to something—a rope—and
whatever rope we have to grab on to, we need to rely on that and
pull ourselves out. We may rely on the Three Jewels,* God, or
the law of karma, or we may simply have a basic trust in the
goodness of the world. Whatever the case, a positive focus
brings stability to our lives and pulls us through challenging
times. Placing our trust in positivity is faith.

We may think that faith is beneath us. We think, "It's
not sophisticated enough; it's too simpleminded." We believe
that faith is blind. People with faith, we believe, are not intelligent thinkers, not philosophically minded. But look honestly:

*The Buddha, Dharma, and Sangha.

Someone may be a sharp thinker, well-read, with a lot of pride in their intelligence, able to say many interesting things at parties, with a lot of charm in the way that they present themselves. But when the shit hits the fan, will their worldly knowledge really sustain them? Not likely. At the end of the day, they will need to cultivate faith. All the brilliant Buddhist scholars of the past, such as Nagarjuna,* have ultimately relied on faith. Saints of all the great traditions have relied on it. We can see how it works in situations where people usually suffer; we see how faith supports them and how it sees them through. The fact that we need a support may be a humbling realization, but if faith can sustain us in this way, how blind can it be?

Recognizing Faith

Most traditions assert that faith finds its origins in an external source. But because faith depends upon our recognition of something positive outside of us, how could it come from an external source alone? Our ability to recognize something greater than ourselves, and value it as a genuine experience, says something about the power, potential, and goodness of our own mind. It says something about the subjective mind— the recognizer—and its capacity to isolate something external and use it to transcend its own small-mindedness. This means that, when we have faith, we place our trust in our own natural intelligence. This natural intelligence has the innate ability to discriminate between something that supports our well-being and something that does not. It connects us to the positivity in the world around us: it brings us to the spiritual path, it brings

---

*An Indian master of the first and second centuries who expounded the teachings of the Middle Way (Madhyamika) school and composed numerous philosophical treatises.

us to our teachers, it allows us to identify the goodness in ourselves and others.

Natural intelligence is an indication of our buddha potential—the cause or seed of our enlightenment. The conditions or contributing factors that nurture the seed, enabling it to sprout, are the external supports, such as the teacher and the teachings. Without these supports, the potential for awakening would simply lie dormant—there would be no way to cultivate it. Although we would continue to strive for happiness and to free ourselves from suffering, we wouldn't have the means to break away from samsara. This is why we need to rely on our natural intelligence and its continuous search, both within and without, for wisdom.

During difficult times we often fail to recognize our wisdom potential because we tend to focus on our pain. At these times we may even feel that faith is not a possibility for us—that it is something that people either have or don't—not something that we can cultivate. But our instinctual longing to experience something beyond pain is nothing other than the call of our Buddha potential, the natural intelligence itself. It is important to recognize this longing and develop some trust in it. It is light coming through.

When we open the shutters on our windows, light streams through, illuminating and beautifying the whole room. The plants in the room always move toward the light; that's why they often grow lopsided, all the branches racing toward a sunny window. This natural movement toward light brings out our own clarity and strength, and so we need to learn to trust it more and more.

TRUST AND DOUBT

Of course, the doubtful mind can mistrust even our direct experiences. For instance, we may momentarily step outside our bubble of self-absorption and have an experience of panoramic awareness, a glimpse of the empty nature of mind or *bodhichitta*. But right away we dismiss it. Somehow the direct experience itself is not enough. We ask, "Where's the proof—the guarantee?" Even if we were to come up with proof, doubt would inevitably distort the facts in some way. Someone might genuinely say, "I love you," but immediately so many doubts arise in our mind: "How much does he love me?" or "Why does she love me?" and so on. We get suspicious and start to make all sorts of comparisons.

Doubt brings up meaninglessness and despair. But rather than being an emotion itself, doubt has to do with wrong views, and this makes it especially difficult to overcome. Emotions are fleeting and irrational. When an emotional storm has settled, things often fall into perspective and make sense again. But doubt continues to undermine our clarity, our instincts, and our own direct experience!

How long can we leave ourselves in a groundless, doubting, nihilistic state and expect to live meaningful lives? People caught in doubt have trouble seeing the possibilities. They think, "If I'm so messed up, everyone and everything else must be messed up too. How can anything possibly be good?" This kind of hopelessness is very big in these modern times. It can really stunt our growth as spiritual practitioners.

Buddhist meditators often experience doubt in their practice. They expect to have strong practice results all of the time and get disheartened when they don't. One of my teachers, Khen Rinpoche, once said that when you put an apple seed in the ground, first a shoot sprouts; we don't expect to see blossoms and apples right away. But the sprout encourages us—from something small, dry, hard, and round emerges a green shoot. It shows us the possibility of a tree. On the spiritual path it is the same. When we apply ourselves, we begin to witness small changes along the way. We may simply hear a teaching on impermanence and see from our own experience that it is true. As we continue to apply the teachings, we begin to also see our mind becoming freer and more wholesome, peaceful, and clear.

When we approach the world through constant probing, continuously asking, "Why, why, why," we keep going around in a circle—we never get anywhere. How can we deepen our understanding in this way? This is the curse of the modern times we live in: We are overwhelmed with too much information. Too much feedback dulls our instincts. The media tells us what we should eat, what we should wear, how we should live, and why we should live that way. So much of the time, we just buy it. We don't take the time to see firsthand whether or not it is true.

Our bodies and minds are always trying to find balance. They have their own natural intelligence. If we eat something, for instance, that throws the body off balance, the body will let us know. We will also feel the wholesome effect of food that is good for us. This is not to say that we should never seek a doctor's advice; it just means that, as the "experiencer," we have a kind of insight into what is happening, one that no one else has. This holds true for all aspects of our life. In our emotional life, our practice life, in our ability to make decisions, what could be more reliable than our own natural intelligence—our own conscience—to guide us through? If we don't take the time to recognize and trust our natural intelligence, who knows where life will take us. If we don't trust our own conscience, who knows what we might start to believe. It is ironic that, although the notion of faith seems so foreign to us, we place our trust in so many things that don't support us at all.

PATRIOTIC VERSUS GENUINE FAITH

When we hold tightly to views without turning to our own wisdom mind, we develop a sort of ego-based faith that you might call patriotic faith. We have faith in *my* country! *My* people! *My* religion! *My* teacher and lineage! We have faith in things because they belong to "me." In truth, such faith doesn't do much for us personally except give us a stronger identity to flash around. When we fall on hard times, this kind of faith doesn't serve us, because it's no more substantial than a puff of smoke in the air. We were so full of ourselves that there really wasn't any room to respect anyone or anything in the first place, it turns out. We get hit hard with the hollowness of our faith and find ourselves as groundless as ever before. Patriotic faith is divisive and produces a lot of zealots. It doesn't have much of a connection to our inner intelligence. It just likes to wave a flag.

Genuine faith isn't based on me and mine. It is an inclusive and open intelligence that is searching for positivity, a sense of ease, an answer to the many questions we have about suffering and happiness. It brings warmth to the heart and makes us feel at home. It is a resting place. It allows us the courage to openly question experience and the world around us. Genuine faith does not require us to put on blinders and believe what we are told. It is an open question. And we can stay open because we trust in something bigger.

11

Working with a Teacher

Not a One-hand Clap

Until we have reached a decision to place our faith in something much greater than our own ego, there is really no point in trying to work with a teacher. The whole point of a spiritual teacher, at least on the Buddhist path to liberation, is to surrender all the ways in which we cherish and protect ourselves. Having seen the pain this produces, we want to give up trying to constantly make everything good for the ego. We want to move away from all the habits that promote the self, and we need some guidance in order to do this. Of course, we have to be ready to accept this guidance.

When we place our trust in a teacher, we let go of the idea of absolute control (not that we ever had it in the first place). From here on in we need to work toward trusting that whatever happens is "good." Not good because that's what we want or good because we are trying to convince ourselves it is good, but good in that, whatever the outcome, we will use it to mature our minds against the ego, which has caused us so much pain and suffering. We have decided to place our trust in the teacher because, through his or her insight into the nature of mind and how it functions, the teacher can support us in achieving this aim.

Before this, when we were only working for our egos, "good" was limited. Good was self-serving and something that didn't get in the way of what *we* wanted to do. Now good is more inclusive because we have let go of trying to control everything and are ready for new experiences. Of course some of these new experiences include ego-disappointment. Ego-disappointment can be a relief . . . that is, if we are motivated by wisdom. Or, if ego has its way with us, it will be a bit traumatic. But, regardless of ego's reaction, there is never a dull moment in working with a teacher. We commit to something much greater than ego, and it's thrilling not to be doing everything in the same old way. The teacher helps direct us toward the things that we have always tried to avoid. Sometimes the teacher directs us toward our own pain. If we want to be an authentic practitioner, we need to understand all aspects of our mind, including the darker and more painful sides.

We may be a reluctant student at first. We're not used to surrendering our egos, with their sneaky little habits and fixations, over to anyone—even if these habits do torture us and make us miserable. When we are resistant, it is hard to trust. But think about it this way: When we are sick, we have no problem relying on a doctor. We even let them cut open our bodies and operate. They take out cancerous tumors and completely remove major organs such as the uterus or gallbladder. They come into the room with their masks and blue pajamas. They turn on bright lights. The nurses wear latex gloves, rushing in and out as if they were in a train station, holding all kinds of sharp instruments. As they put us to sleep, we wonder if we will ever get up again! But we allow ourselves to be that vulnerable because we want to get healthy.

Compared to all of this, the teacher's advice is gentle. The medicine the teacher gives, the *buddhadharma*, cures the most serious illness—self-importance and ignorance. Its purpose is to soothe. The Dharma teaches that even pain—that which we fear most—is nothing but thought and sensation. So we learn it's really not sensation that torments us but instead our fear of letting go and having a new experience. Some people can take the risk of letting go based on trust and others not. Some are too attached to self. Others know that this will simplify their life and put their mind at ease. Our success is determined by how much trust we have in our mind—trusting what mind can do— how it can face pain and how wisdom can come from that. If we follow the Dharma, liberation is at our fingertips. So we really have no reason to hesitate.

Bringing the student along the path toward liberation is the deepest wish of an authentic teacher. So, if we are ready, it can work. It's a choice that we make—a choice to surrender and to trust. When we are able to surrender, we immediately feel the strength of it inside.

The Purpose of the Teacher

When we begin to study with a teacher, we are attracted to his or her qualities. Most likely these qualities have inspired us to go further with our spiritual path. At the same time we don't understand everything about the teacher's mind or realization— we have just begun to engage in Dharma studies and experience meditation practice ourselves. So the teacher's mind and the teachings will be a bit of a mystery to us, and that's natural.

At the same time, there should not be a lot of mystique around our intention to study with a teacher. We should know why we want to embark on the path and what the purpose of a teacher is. If we leave our motivation vague, we might continue to expect things from the teacher that he or she cannot give. It will be like a one-handed clap. The teacher will be teaching and trying to guide us along the path, and we will be expecting something else . . . maybe an ordinary friendship . . . maybe we will be looking for someone to inspire us or tend to our emotional needs . . . maybe a mother or a father.

Sometimes a student will say, "I want to trust and surrender my ego . . . but I need to know that you will catch me if I fall." They fear that letting go might be like mining for gold and only finding ordinary rock. The student asks for an emotional guarantee from the teacher, as if he or she is about to sacrifice something very sacred and precious in order to become a student. I think there is some misunderstanding in this kind of approach. First of all, what we need to surrender is not something sacred or precious at all—it is the ego—the root of all our misery. So in surrendering the ego, the student is the primary beneficiary. And because surrendering ego brings peace, the "sacrifice" *itself* is the liberation.

If we don't understand this point, it would almost seem as if we, the student, expected the teacher to become our emotional pacemaker. In other words, we could feel that if the teacher doesn't continually inspire us and tend to our emotional needs, our hearts may very well stop beating. But there is some misunderstanding in this kind of approach. As the Buddha himself said, "I will show you the way, but liberation depends on you." This makes clear, I think, what the dynamic between teacher and student should be.

Without this understanding there is no context for anything beneficial to take place between a teacher and student. We may study and practice the teachings, and they may penetrate a bit, but if we don't want to relate to our obscurations, and refuse to believe they are even there, no spiritual development can take place. Without the proper motivation to guide and protect us, we will want to get enmeshed just as we do in all of our ordinary relationships. Meanwhile the teacher will just be waiting . . . waiting . . . waiting for the day we decide to surrender to wisdom rather than ignorance.

The motivation of any authentic teacher arises from the principles of *bodhichitta*. The teacher wants to benefit the students, for sure. At the same time I don't know of any teacher that is constantly tormented by or loses sleep over how much a student does or doesn't practice or adhere to their vows, how much they respect the laws of karma or study their texts. The whole point is for us to engage our studies and practice to benefit our own minds, not the teacher. So again, we need to understand the true purpose of the teacher. Otherwise we will be like a child eating our vegetables as if we were doing our mom a big favor . . . and this just isn't the case.

The Kindness of the Teacher

It is said, "Always remember the kindness of the teacher." The teacher shows us how to liberate our minds, releasing all our innate qualities such as compassion, strength, fearlessness, and wisdom. But the way the teacher is kind might not always be all sunny days and soothing words the way the ego would like. If the teacher were always sunshine and we always just felt moved and touched—even to the point of having tears constantly welling up in our eyes and dripping down our face—nothing would develop. In fact our ego would just get more and more self-satisfied.

Fortunately, we join forces with the teacher to snub out the ego and reduce it to dust. So we can expect the teacher to relate to us with strength and clarity that help us let go of ordinary mind and fixation. Together we commit to scrutinizing the ego for the sake of our well-being. If we just want to consult with the teacher or vent our emotional difficulties but don't really want to hear his or her honest feedback, there is no point in having a teacher in the first place. So we really need to be open.

Sure, there may be times we want to run away . . . but hiding won't help, and we know that. There's no way to escape our own mind. So, again, we have to reflect on the nature of the relationship and get to work. This is the greatest project on earth and the more passionate we get about it the better. There's always something helpful to expose to our awareness—a hindrance, a blind spot, something to purify or to realize and appreciate. There is always room to grow, which means we never have to feel disappointed in what we find.

When we can use all our experience to progress on the path—when it becomes "all good"—nothing can sway us from our intention. Our sense of trust needs to be unshakeable and unconditional, which means not based on outer causes and conditions. All the great practitioners of the past and present have had this kind of conviction. Having to face your ego is not a curse on you; it is the greatest of all blessings, and good news for us if we can get beyond the mundane way of thinking about it.

THE GREAT JOINT VENTURE

When I was young I often felt challenged by my teacher's command or simply by his presence or what I sometimes perceived as his displeasure. Sometimes it was just his silence, or he would look at me with a certain deep penetration. Sometimes I wondered whether it was actually his intention to challenge me. Of course, sometimes my teacher did have something to point out. But, in retrospect, I know a lot of it was my own mind projected onto the teacher. In fact, I was dealing with my own mind and its habits, including negative habits that I was not ready to give up, even though they were dragging me down. There was a dualism going on in my mind: I wanted to be a good student but then found out that I was not so good after all; I wanted to impress the teacher but was not able to because I could not free myself of certain thoughts and emotions.

A few times I thought my teacher was quite upset with me, but when I looked into it further, I found that he had no judgment whatsoever. At first I was terrified he might confront me. But my teacher's mind was so spacious, which made me understand that whatever I was fixated on wasn't such a big deal for him. Whenever I could remember that, I felt a deep sense of the teacher's acceptance, love, and care, like you would feel from a mother. But it was more than a mother's care. There was not only acceptance, but a sense of openness and wakefulness.

As the relationship with the teacher matures, there develops a sense of being a team, a sense of kinship. In my case, it was truly a delight to discuss the Dharma, to learn more about how to practice the Dharma. At that point, it's not one person trying to teach another. Both parties share the same vision. At this point I was able to see my teacher's deep appreciation for Dharma and his 100 percent conviction in its ability to bring sentient beings to a state of liberation. I felt great joy in sharing that with him. When this happens, your love for Dharma begins to equal the teacher's love of Dharma, and that becomes the basis for deep kinship. It is not that I saw myself as equal to the teacher or that I had nothing left to learn. I actually felt more appreciation than ever before. It's just that it was no longer a one-handed clap. . . . We were both on the same page.

12

Devotion and Lineage

From the Womb of the Mother

Not everyone finds interest in surrendering to a teacher. Not everyone feels inclined to take that step. People do what they wish. But perhaps there are some individuals who want to fully embody the wisdom of Dharma, so for them devotion is a good topic to speak on. I know that sometimes talk of devotion scares people. Yet these things must be said, if not simply for the record. Dharma is just evolving in the West and taking many forms. We are searching for ways to integrate Dharma into our culture and make it accessible. But whatever the culture— whether it be here in the West, in India, or in Tibet—the traditional methods remain the same. We need to be clear on this.

CULTIVATED AND EFFORTLESS DEVOTION

During the early stages of our Buddhist path, we spend a lot of time and effort trying to understand how to support our path through our connection with the teacher. We wonder, "What is devotion, and how can I cultivate it?" Sometimes devotion seems to arise naturally without deliberate effort. Other times we need to cultivate or shape our devotion through reflecting upon the importance of the teacher, through service, or through engaging in practices, such as prostrations and supplication. Learning how to shape our mind in this way is part of our natural growth process as practitioners, providing that we see the wisdom in it. Cultivated devotion wouldn't actually serve us if we didn't understand its importance to our path and its potential to support and transform our mind.

As the teachings gradually become more deeply rooted in our own direct experience, we begin to feel the warmth and blessings of the practice. During the moments when this happens, a natural or uncultivated devotion, one that is genuine and heartfelt, wells up effortlessly from within. Due to the teacher's unparalleled kindness, we begin to emerge from our own suffering and confusion. At these times, gratitude is not something we have to cultivate. It happens on its own. It would be similar to someone having saved our lives. If someone were to save our life, chances are, we wouldn't have to conjure up appreciation.

INSEPARABILITY

As our natural appreciation grows, we begin to perceive the nature of the guru's mind and our own as inseparable. It is not as if the student's nature is inferior and the teacher's nature is superior. The student realizes that his or her own wisdom potential is inseparable from the teacher's, which comes from the same source as the wisdom of all the buddhas.

At a certain point on the Buddhist path, strong spiritual practitioners become so familiar with the nature of their own mind that they don't have to look outside of themselves for something to rely on. For them everything resolves into the equal nature of one-taste, and so, no matter what arises, they feel at ease. They don't have aversion or attachment to any particular state of mind. Whatever arises, they simply rest in that view. If shakiness or uncertainty arise, it simply enhances their practice, so they welcome the challenge. But just because the student has realized the inseparability of his or her mind with the teacher's, don't think for a moment that the student forgets where this realization came from.

The Teacher as the Source of Realization

Once my teacher, Dilgo Khyentse Rinpoche, received a commentary on a text about buddha nature, written by his teacher Shechen Gyaltsab Rinpoche. This particular commentary was unavailable in Nepal or India at the time. When Tibet opened up a bit, and people could get access to books that were stored there, this text was brought to him. When it arrived, he stood up and went outside the monastery to receive it. Then he brought it in, placed it on the throne, and began to prostrate. While he prostrated, he just broke down and cried, cried from his heart for some time. I feel moved when I think of my teacher expressing his deep devotion and appreciation in this way.

This kind of devotion comes when a genuine appreciation for the teacher and the teachings has deeply penetrated our ignorance. We have experienced the hardships of breaking through our own confusion, and we know that it could never have happened without the teacher. I knew that my teacher was definite about his liberation—where it came from—and his connection to his teacher. When we reach this point, our devotion will reflect this clearly. We won't simply assume that realization occurs by accident, that we somehow hit the enlightenment jackpot, or that it was simply due to our own hard work, our own special qualities, and so on. When a mother gives birth to a child, there is no mistaking where the baby came from. It is evident that the child emerged from the womb of the mother. Whatever happens thereafter, that will always be true.

All the great lineage masters have regarded their teachers with tremendous humility and appreciation. You can read story after story in the texts. All of these realized beings were independent as practitioners, fully confident in the view of the practice. Yet all of them attributed their realization to their teachers. This may seem dualistic to some. One might ask, "If we can realize the true nature of our own mind, why continue to supplicate an external teacher?" But there is no contradiction here. We can have an experience of the nature of our mind that is completely unobstructed and unconfused, while at the same time having a profound feeling of appreciation for the source of our awakening.

Lineage of Realization

Passing down the essence of the teachings—from teacher to student—is lineage. A student can spend a lifetime collecting teachings and counting mantras, but that alone won't do it. The student must develop the proper attitude and motivation. This attitude is cultivated through the instructions of the teacher and the teachings. But more than that, it has to do with how open or devoted you are and how much realization you have. This realization is information for yourself—it benefits you. It's not something to proclaim to the teacher so that he or she knows how "devoted" you are. It has to do with where you are, what you are doing with your life, how far you have come, and how far you want to go in realizing the nature of your mind and its inseparability with the teacher's. This is how a lineage is maintained.

We have a saying in Tibetan: "The qualities of a statue depend on how good the mold is." One mold won't produce a variety of statues. Thinking that everyone has to be individual or unique is a modern idea: it doesn't embody the spirit of humility and appreciation at the heart of the lineage. So, although we may like to think otherwise, the nature of our wisdom—or our ignorance—is not all that unique. In fact, the sameness, or universality, of our experience makes the teachings applicable for everyone.

If the teachings are precise, then the way the student follows them will be precise. In turn, the student's experience will be precise, and so the wisdom will dawn just as it always has. This is not to say, of course, that people don't have different personalities and approaches. Some teachers take a more scholarly approach, others prefer to spend their time in retreat and benefit through example, while others employ less conventional means. But when it comes to realization itself and how it unfolds from within, there is no difference whatsoever. It is not as if one teacher has an eccentric realization while another has a more conservative realization or that one is superior to another's. There may be a difference in depth—how far they have come—but not in the essential qualities of the nature of realization itself.

Part Three

TEACHINGS
ON EMPTINESS

13

Mere Appearance

Thinking like an Elephant

Recently a close friend and old student of mine was diag nosed with cancer. When I visit him, I see him sorting out his situation. He's thinking about his life, the time he has left, and how he would like to die. I think, "Roy is here now; I don't know how long he will be here. What will it be like when he is gone?" I think of my own death. We all have to die. We don't know when. These kinds of situations shake us out of the habit of going about our daily business without giving death much thought.

We hold strongly to existence. We think, because there is "me," there is the extinction of "me." Because there is "mine," there is the extinction of "mine." Even if we believe in reincarnation, we still have this sense of "me" to contend with, the "me" that continues and experiences whatever comes next. But before our next rebirth, what we think of as "me" is severed from everything that defines it—its body, all of its characteristics and possessions, its friends and loved ones. This is the loss of "mine." So even after death the pain of "me" and "mine," and of the extinction of "me" and "mine," continues.

The ordinary dualistic mind is limited to thinking in the extremes of existence or nonexistence. We believe phenomena—

97

including our "selves"—exist objectively from their own side as independent and autonomous things. This is not merely philosophical. Most likely it's not philosophical at all, or even conscious. This is how we emotionally and viscerally experience our life and our world.

If we were to see, for instance, "me" in a broader way—an interdependent way—the self would lose its distinction as a solid, individual entity. We would experience the self as less contracted and separate from everything else, as a dynamic that changes and interacts with other elements, so our experience of everything would become more open and relaxed. But this broad way of looking is not our habitual approach. Habitually we hold to a sense of autonomy. We don't usually see the constantly changing components and the various causes and conditions that underlie that sense of autonomy.

When we hold to existence in this way, it seems we have to succumb to extinction. Something must necessarily become nothing in the end: a void—complete annihilation. "Here today, gone tomorrow," as they say. What other alternative to existence could there be? The great nineteenth-century Tibetan-Buddhist scholar Mipham Rinpoche describes this type of dualistic thinking in the following example: "Conventional mind is like an elephant who bathes in the water to wash off the dirt, and then rolls in the dirt to dry off."

This kind of dualism penetrates not only our core views; it penetrates our peripheral daily experiences too—small things. Thinking that things exist objectively and independently invites fear into our lives. There is so much to cherish and protect. We have so many preferences, hopes, and fears. We always get snagged by one shenpa or another. Our shenpas makes us feel that we can't accommodate the challenges in life. We are haunted by the truth of impermanence, that we have to die, that there is so much loss and suffering to come, that things might not work out as we wish, that we might lose what we have. Fearing we can't handle these challenges is a privileged attitude. We cannot pick and choose the things that arise in our lives. We really have no choice.

Of course we hold on anyway. As humans we are incredibly innovative and creative in the way we do this. Shenpas run deep. We experience the heavy "realness" of clinging. We interpret this realness as things harassing us from the outside—all those intrinsic objects, all those real thoughts and emotions. When our bodies get sick, the sickness binds us. When our thoughts disturb us, they bind us and threaten us because we experience a sense of emotional and physical intrinsic essentialness, which seems to come from the object itself. But does it?

Have You Ever Really Seen One?

Ask yourself, "Have you ever really seen an intrinsic thing?" The notion that something could exist from its own side, disconnected from everything else, is absurd and impossible to even imagine. Can we point to a phenomenon that is not made of parts and that is not dependent on other elements to come into being? It is not something we have ever experienced or will ever encounter. Even the moment we try to imagine something, we create a relationship of dependence with it. The state of essentialness would, by virtue of its unchanging nature, be a state of being that is completely not experienced by any kind of awareness whatsoever. It would have to exist in complete isolation from everything else. Who could ever say that such a thing exists? And if nothing exists intrinsically how can we speak of a thing that is intrinsically nonexisent? Although we do not or cannot actually experience phenomena as intrinsically existent or nonexistent we cling to them as if they were.

How do we experience phenomena? We see that phenomena arise and dissolve. We see things change. As individuals, we are not static and are far from being autonomous. It would be impossible to count the causes and conditions that brought us into existence. It would be impossible to count the components of our experience at any given moment: the momentariness of our thoughts and perceptions or the subtle elements of our physical being. A moment itself is made of parts, but these parts themselves don't linger for even an instant. There's nothing we can point to and say, "Aha! There's one!" By the time that thought has a chance to occur, whatever we were pointing to will have vanished. Try that and see.

We can attribute all these relationships, all this motion, change, and unfindability, to the natural law of interdependence. It is simply because things arise interdependently that we can ever experience them at all. If things lingered in a static state—for even a static moment—as I said before, we wouldn't experience them. For this reason, holding to them as real and autonomous is a mistake of our conceptual and emotional being.

Existence and nonexistence are nothing more than conceptual contrivances. In other words, these views—whether we cling to them in a philosophical way or an unconscious emotional way—are extraneous to the nature of things. They exist only as imputations. Clinging to a "me" where there is no "me" is an exaggeration. The exaggeration is the experience of essentialness we feel—the sense of solid "me-ness," when, in fact, there is no entity "me" to be found. This is not to deny the appearance and function of "me"—to reduce it to dust. Not finding an intrinsic entity is not a denial of what we experience in the least. Appearance is not in question here. What is in question is phenomena's true mode of being. We are looking at the discrepancy between the way things appear to us and the way they actually are.

THE BUDDHA'S MIDDLE WAY

Phenomena may appear to us as solid and real, but, because they are dependent, we cannot say they exist from their own side. In this way, phenomena lack true existence. On the other hand, phenomena appear to our senses and conceptual mind, and they function through their dependence on "other." In this way we cannot say that phenomena are nonexistent. Understanding that phenomena are beyond both existence and nonexistence brings us to the Buddha's Middle Way.* Phenomena are illusory like a dream, a rainbow, or a magical display. They *merely* appear. They appear, and yet we can't point to their characteristics and say that something exists independent of its parts in a singular or intrinsic way.

What does this realization affect? It affects our fears. It affects the way we relate to life and therefore the way we relate to death. So when I think of my friend, I've been asking myself, "Who is Roy?" Roy is a loving father in relation to his daughters. He is a loyal husband in relation to his wife. He is a faithful son in relation to his parents. He is a devoted student in relation to his teacher. He is a friend, a member of a spiritual community, and a dharma brother. He is a businessman in relation to his work and a practitioner in relation to his spiritual path. His body is composed of blood, flesh, and bone, which in

---

*The Middle Way is a Buddhist philosophical view.

turn are comprised of the elements of space, the air of his lungs, heat, water, and matter. These inner elements mingle with the outer elements that support his body: the food he eats and the elements that compose it, the space he moves about in, the air he breathes. He is a speck in the universe. He is the master of his own universe. Roy is part of everything, yet where is he? And if we can't find Roy how can we speak of the extinction of Roy?

Realizing interdependence leads us to the naked understanding of reality beyond the extremes of existence and nonexistence—reality empty of all conceptual contrivances. A disciple of the Buddha once asked him, "What is emptiness?" The Buddha then entered the nonverbal state of meditation. Manjushri* explained that this was the Buddha's expression free of all contrivances, a state of non-grasping and freedom from shenpa. There is not much to say about the nature of emptiness. The only characteristic you could say it possesses is a freedom from all characteristics. If you want to know more about the meaning of emptiness, you'll have to sit on your cushion and find out for yourself.

*The bodhisattva of wisdom.

14

The Haunted Dominion
of the Mind

Shaken from Within

In old Tibet, practitioners went to charnel grounds, springs, haunted houses, haunted trees, and so on in order to reveal how deeply their practice had cut to the core of their fears and attachments. The practice of cutting through our deepest attachments and fears to their core is called *nyensa chodpa*, which means "cutting through the haunted dominion of the mind." It is not that I am encouraging you to go to these haunted places to test yourself, but the view behind *nyensa chodpa* is important for all practitioners to understand, because until we are challenged, we don't know how deep our practice has gone.

We may be established practitioners. We may be comfortable with our practice and working with our minds; everything could be going smoothly. As my teacher Kyabje Dilgo Khyentse Rinpoche used to say, "Practice is easy when the sun is on your back and your belly is full." But when difficult circumstances arise and we are completely shaken from within, when we hit rock bottom, when something is haunting us and we feel completely vulnerable and exposed to all our neuroses, then it's a different story.

Challenging circumstances expose to us how much we have learned from studying and practicing the *buddhadharma* and how much we have learned from our meditation practice and the experience of our mind. But we don't need to place ourselves in challenging external circumstances to uncover our hidden fears and attachments. We don't need to wait for our bliss bubble to pop, for a dear one to die, or to find out we have a fatal disease. There is plenty of opportunity to practice *nyensa chodpa* right here in our own minds. There is plenty of opportunity because there is plenty of self-clinging.

The haunted dominion of mind is the dominion of self-clinging. It is the world of self and all the hopes and fears that come with trying to secure it. Our efforts to secure the self give rise to all the negative emotions. If we were not so concerned with cherishing and providing for the self, there would be no reason for attachment. Aggression, too, would have no reason to arise if there were no self to protect. And jealousy, which shows up whenever we think the self is lacking something, would have no impetus to eat away at our inner peace because we would be content with the natural richness and confidence of our own mind. If we had no need to shield all of the embarrassing things about the self that make us so insecure, we would have no cause for arrogance. Finally, if we were not so fixated on the self, we could rely on our innate intelligence rather than letting our stupidity escort us through the same activities that bring us so much pain time and time again.

So emotions themselves are not the cause of the problem. Yet, until we reach down to the very root of our negative emotions, they will be there, standing in line, waiting to "save" us from our fundamental insecurities. Unless we let go of grasping to the self with all its egotistical scheming, all this trying to figure out how to save the self in the usual manner, we will only continue to enforce a stronger and stronger belief in the solidity of the self. If the aim of practice is to free ourselves from our endless insecurities, then we must cut through self-clinging. Until we do, self-clinging will define our relationship with the world, whether it be the inner world of our own mind or the world outside of us.

From the perspective of the self, the world is either for us or against us. If it is for us, its purpose is to feed our infinite attachments. If it is against us, it is to be rejected and it adds to our infinite paranoia. It is either our friend or our enemy, something to lure in or reject. The stronger we cling to a self, the stronger our belief grows in a solid, objective world that exists separate from us. The more we see it as solid and separate, the more the world haunts us: we are haunted by what we want from the world, and we are haunted by our struggle to protect ourselves from it.

THE MOVEMENT OF THE ENTIRE UNIVERSE

The many problems we see in the larger world today, and also encounter in our own personal lives, spring from the belief that the enemy or threat is outside of us. This split occurs when we forget how deeply connected we are to others and the world around us. This is not to say that mind and the phenomenal world are one and that everything we experience is a mere figment of our imagination. It simply means that what we believe to be a self and what we believe to be other than self are inextricably linked and that, in truth, the self can only exist in relation to other. Seeing them as separate is really the most primitive way of viewing and engaging our lives.

To see the connectedness or interdependence of all things is to see in a big way. It reduces the artificial separation we create between the self and everything else. For instance, when we hold tightly to a self, the natural law of impermanence looms as a threat to our existence. But when we accept that we are part of this natural flow, we begin to see that the entity we cling to as a static, immutable, and independent self is just a continuous stream of experience comprised of thoughts, feelings, forms, and perceptions that change moment to moment. When we accept this, we become part of something much greater—the movement of the entire universe.

What we experience as "my life" results from the interdependent relationship between the outer world—the world of color, shape, sound, smell, taste, and touch—and our awareness. We cannot separate awareness—the knower—from that which is known. Is it possible, for instance, to see without a visual object or to hear without a sound? And how can we isolate the content of our thoughts from the information we receive from our environment, our relationships, and the imprints of our sense perceptions? How can we separate our body from the elements that comprise it or the food we eat to keep us alive or the causes and conditions that brought our body into existence?

In fact there is little consistency in what we consider to be self and what we consider to be other. Sometimes we include our emotions as part of the self. Other times our anger or depression seems to haunt or even threaten us. Our thoughts, too, seem to define who we are as individuals, but so often they agitate or excite us as if they existed as other. Generally we identify the body with the self, yet when we fall ill, we often find ourselves saying, "My stomach is bothering me," or, "My liver is giving me trouble." If we investigate carefully, we will inevitably conclude that to pinpoint where the self leaves off and the world begins is not really possible. The one thing we can observe is that everything that arises, both what we consider to be the self and what we consider to be other than self, does so through a relationship of interdependence.

THE SINGULAR NATURE OF EMPTINESS

All phenomena depend upon other in order to arise, express themselves, and fall away. There is nothing that can be found to exist on its own, independent and separate from everything else. That self and other lack clearly defined boundaries does not then mean that we are thrown into a vague state of not knowing who we are and how to relate to the world, or that we lose our discerning intelligence. It simply means that through loosening the clinging we have to our small, constricted notion of self, we begin to relax into the true nature of all phenomena: the non-dual state of emptiness that transcends both self and other.

Having gone beyond dualistic mind, we can enjoy the "single unit" of our own profound *dharmakaya* nature.* The singularity of emptiness is not single as opposed to many. It is a state beyond one or two, beyond subject and object, and the self and the world outside; it is the singular nature of all things. Upon recognizing the nature of emptiness, our own delusion—the false duality of subject and object—cracks apart and dissolves. This relieves us of the heaviness produced by the subtle underlying belief that things have a separate or solid nature. At the same time we apprehend the interconnectedness of everything, and this gives a greater vision to our lives.

*The empty nature of all phenomena.

CONVICTION

Cultivating a deep conviction in the view of emptiness is what the practice of *nyensa chodpa* is all about. *Nyensa* refers to that which haunts us: our clinging to the self and all the fears and delusion this produces. *Chodpa* means "to cut through." What is it that cuts through our clinging, fears, and delusion? It is the realization of emptiness, the realization of the truth. When the view of emptiness dawns in our experience, if even only for a moment, self-grasping naturally dissolves. This is when we begin to develop confidence in what is truly possible.

Impressed by the great Tibetan yogi Milarepa's unwavering confidence in the view of emptiness, the Ogress of the Rock, while attempting to haunt and frighten him, made this famous statement, which illustrates the view of *nyensa chodpa* very well. She said,

> This demon of your own tendencies arises from your
> mind. If you don't recognize the [empty] nature of
> your mind, I'm not going to leave just because you tell
> me to go. If you don't realize that your mind is empty,
> there are many more demons besides myself. But if you
> recognize the [empty] nature of your own mind, ad-
> verse circumstances will serve only to sustain you, and
> even I, Ogress of the Rock, will be at your bidding.*

To understand emptiness conceptually is not enough. We need to understand it through direct experience, so that, when we are shaken from the depth of our being, when the whole

*Quoted in Patrul Rinpoche, *The Words of My Perfect Teacher*, trans. Padmakara Translation Group (New York: HarperCollins, 1994), p. 206.

mechanism of self-clinging is challenged, we can rest in this view with confidence. When challenging circumstances arise, we cannot just conceptually patch things up with the ideas we have about emptiness. Merely thinking, "Everything is empty," does little service at such times. It is like walking into a dimly lit room, seeing a rope on the ground, and mistaking it for a snake. We can tell ourselves, "It's a rope, it's a rope, it's a rope," all we want, but unless we turn on the light and see for ourselves, we will never be convinced it is not a snake and our fear will remain. When we turn on the light, we can see through direct experience that what we mistook as a snake was actually a rope, and our fear lifts. In the same way, when we realize the empty nature of the self and the world around us, we free ourselves from the clinging and fear that comes with it. It is essential that we have conviction based upon experience, no matter how great or small that experience is.

Without this conviction we may run up against a lot of doubts about our meditation practice when difficult circumstances surface. We may wonder why our meditation isn't working. If meditation does not serve us in difficult times, what else can we do to rescue ourselves from the horror and fear we have inside? We think to ourselves, what about all the years of practice we have done? Were we just fooling ourselves; was our practice ever genuine at all?

In times like these, we need not get discouraged about our ability to practice. Coupled with open-minded questioning, challenging circumstances can help deepen and clarify the purpose of our path because they expose how far our practice has penetrated to the core of self-clinging. Although these experiences often shock or disturb us, they bring our attention to the immediate experience of clinging and the pain it generates, and we begin to think about letting go.

We may have had the experience of letting go of our clinging and resting in the nature of emptiness many times in the
past but not yet developed the trust or conviction in that experience. In the moment that our ordinary, confused perceptions
collapse, we may feel some certainty. But unless we trust that
experience, it will not affect the momentum of our ordinary,
confused habits. Quickly we will return to believing in our experience as solid and real. However, if we are able to trust the
direct experience of emptiness, we can, through hindsight,
bridge that understanding with our present experience. We
rely on the recollection of our direct encounter with the view
to change the way we ordinarily respond to difficult situations.

On the other hand, even if we do have some conviction, it is
not as if, because we have let go once—"That's it!"—we've let
go completely, and we will never cling again. Habitual mind is
like a scroll of paper: When you first unroll it, it curls back up
immediately. You need to continually flatten it out, and eventu-
ally it will stay. Reducing the attachment we have in the core of
our mind is our constant challenge as practitioners—the true
focus of our practice.

As we approach the haunted dominion with less fear, we
may actually find some intelligence in the experience of being
haunted: Although we continuously try to secure the self, we
instinctually know that we cannot. This instinctual knowledge
comes from an innate intelligence that sees the dynamic, un-
graspable nature of all things. It observes things arise and fall
away, both happiness and suffering, and the changes of birth,
old age, sickness, and death. When we cling to self and other,
our mind feels deeply conflicted and fearful because clinging is
at odds with our inner intelligence. Of course, we are not clinging because we want to suffer; we are clinging because we want
to avoid suffering. But clinging, by its nature, causes pain.

When we let go of grasping and turn toward our innate intelligence, we begin to experience a sense of ease in our minds, and we begin to develop a new relationship with that which ordinarily haunts us.

As practitioners interested in going beyond delusion, we may find ourselves intrigued by the haunted dominion of mind. We may find that rather than trying to avoid pain, we want to move closer to that which haunts us. Emboldened by the experience of emptiness, we can question the solidity or truth of our fears—maybe things don't exist as they appear. In fact, each time we see through the haunted dominion of mind—when we see its illusory or empty nature—we experience the taste of true liberation. This is why the great yogis of the past practiced in haunted places such as charnel grounds. Places that provoke the hidden aspects of mind are full of possibilities for liberation. In this way the haunted dominion—whether it be a charnel ground or the dominion of fear that results from our own self-clinging—serves as the very ground of our realization.

What Is Truly Possible

We don't need to cling to the self to enjoy life. Life is naturally rich and abundant. There is nothing more liberating and enjoyable than experiencing the world around us without grasping. We do not deprive ourselves of experience if we forsake our attachments. Clinging actually inhibits us from enjoying life to its fullest. We consume ourselves trying to arrange the world according to our preferences rather than delighting in the way our experience naturally unfolds.

We can find so much appreciation of life when we are free of the hopes and fears related to self-clinging; we can appreciate even all the problems we generally try to avoid and that we dread, such as old age, sickness, and death. The ability to appreciate all aspects of our mind really says something about mind's magnificent potential. It shows us that the mind is so much greater than the confusions, fears, and unrest that so often haunt us. It shows us that our personal suffering and the world of suffering outside of us are nothing more than the inner and outer world of our own delusion—samsara.

Nyensa chodpa is cutting through the mind of samsara. What could be more haunted and fearful than samsara? What could be a greater benefit than getting beyond samsara and our own self-grasping? What could be more meaningful than recognizing that samsara—that which has made us so fearful and shaken—is in essence the non-dual nature of emptiness itself? If we can do the practice of *nyensa chodpa* in our own everyday life, it would be a wonderful way to live this life, and the work we do will measure up in the end.

15

The "Unfindability" of Phenomena

Disassembling Delusion

The practice of Buddhism has two approaches to the ultimate nature of phenomena. One has to do with disassembling delusion through an analytical investigation of mind and experience. As we examine our experience conceptually through the wisdom of Dharma, we begin to move toward the realization that there is nothing to disassemble. Once we develop confidence through investigation, we can let our conceptual mind disassemble itself. Through letting any thoughts, emotions, and physical sensations we may encounter arise and dissolve, we can experience the natural state free of conceptual contrivances. This second kind of practice requires that we let go of all effort, allowing everything to be as it is.

An unexamined mind takes all experiences at face value. The way we perceive phenomena is gross and bewildered. Yes, of course we can keep our job and our life in order. But we so often feel an underlying anxiety that we are not in control. We don't feel completely at ease with our mind, our thoughts, and our emotions. And if we were to sit quietly with our thoughts for a few hours, without any clarity of how to let them arise and dissolve, we would most likely get overwhelmed. Because of this we can't expect to simply relax in the natural state of mind without doing a bit of groundwork first.

Disassembling delusion means taking apart conceptual mind. To do this, we need to closely investigate and refine our understanding of the components of our experience: consciousness and objects. Consciousness always arises in dependence upon an object; we can't speak of perception without an object,* nor can we experience anything without being conscious of it. Can we have a conscious experience of a mango, for instance, without a mango . . . or at least an imaginary picture of a mango? And who can speak of a mango without a consciousness perceiving it? Mind and experience are not two separate things. Subject and object arise in dependence upon each other, and not in a static way, but in a manner of constant movement and change—a momentary succession of experiences.

We look at a mango. The mango has many qualities—it is spherical and slightly irregular. We see its texture and smoothness, its various colors: shades of yellow, red, orange, and green. We smell its ripeness. We seem to perceive all of these qualities in one instant of awareness, but, in actuality, perception takes place in a sequence of subtle flickering moments. The eye perceives yellow in a separate moment from red, separate from orange and green. It perceives the texture of the mango as distinct from the perception of its shape, and it perceives the way the light reflects on the mango as separate still. The information we receive through our senses is a subtle, rapidly moving continuum. And although our sense perceptions take in this momentariness, the conceptual mind misses it completely. We see an object and immediately think, "It's a mango." But, in fact, if

---

*"Objects" here refers to physical objects, imaginary objects, or previous thoughts.

everything happened at once, as we seem to encounter it, we wouldn't experience the discrete qualities of anything, and we wouldn't be able to describe the mango in the way that we do. Without momentariness we would never experience change: an unripe mango would never ripen; a sprout would never follow a seed; day would never follow night; experience wouldn't move along . . . and that wouldn't be good, because, after all, life must go on!

ONE-SIXTIETH OF A SECOND

The Abhidharma, the corpus of the Buddha's teachings that explains the phenomenal world, states that we experience phenomena as a succession of rapid flashes of consciousness, each one-sixtieth of a second in duration. In each fraction of a second, subject and object come together. The eye consciousness meets the red of the mango . . . the yellow . . . the green. It is not unlike a movie. When we watch a movie, what seems like a "smooth ride" is just a succession of flashing lights flickering twenty-four frames per second. We don't consciously experience the intervals of darkness between frames, but scientists can physically measure certain areas of the brain responding to the flickering of these frames of light. While our sense perceptions receive subtle information, conceptual mind assembles and packages this information, organizing and labeling it. The result is that we experience phenomena in a less subtle and more condensed and gross way.

The earth is over three billion years old, the universe older. But from the Buddhist perspective, nothing lasts longer than one-sixtieth of a second.* So from the point of view of the way

*Mahayana Buddhists accept momentariness, or impermanence, as a relative truth but not an absolute truth.

phenomena seem to arise, we experience everything in its moment. If we look at any given moment, we see that the past moment has dissolved and the future has not yet arisen. We can't see yesterday or tomorrow in today. We can't see the previous hour or the next hour in this hour, or the previous or next minute in the present one. So however ancient we think life, the world, or the universe may be, it is always a unique and fresh moment.

THE LAST BREATH OF DELUSION

Now as long as we can label something as a moment—a single unit of time—it can be broken.* Even one-sixtieth of a second has a past, present, and future. As long as we can point to *something*—even if the experience of that something lingers for only a fraction of a second—it is compounded and can be broken down. We can continue to deconstruct our concept of time in this way until we find no past, present, or future—no final unit of time. If there is no final unit of time, when and where does experience take place?

Observing that things don't linger even momentarily, we may wonder how they appear, and consequently arrive at the conclusion that appearances must arise and cease simultaneously. This is the last breath of delusion, the tail end of the belief in something occurring. If we can't find anything that abides, how can we even say something arises and ceases simultaneously? With one small step forward, this vague sense of

---

*The proponents of the foundational, or Hinayana, schools accept momentariness as the absolute truth. The Mahayana school refutes this by saying that as long as we impute an existence onto anything, even a fraction of a moment, it is compounded and can be broken. Mayahana schools accept momentariness as an accurate and refined understanding of the relative truth, but they only accept emptiness as the absolute truth itself.

some entity that seems to arise and cease at the same time becomes unfindable. This can be a conceptual experience. It can also be the direct experience of our timeless nature. This moves us from knowledge to wisdom, from conceptual mind to direct experience, from effort to effortlessness, from momentariness to timelessness.

THE TIMELESS NATURE

We may feel that this process of disassembling the continuum of appearance is like mentally annihilating the phenomenal world. But we should get clear on why we employ this method of analysis: its purpose is to disassemble the ignorance that sees things in a gross or solid way and blinds us to our timeless nature. We are always in this state of timelessness, whether we can recognize it or not. The phenomenal world, by its nature, has always been and will always be uncompounded. The nature of things can never be altered nor can we alter it. Appearance never binds us. What binds us is our grasping to appearance as solid and real. So whether our mind functions within the realm of time or not, whether we grasp to appearance as solid or not, and whether we are conscious that phenomena are compounded or not, we always truly operate from within our timeless nature.

EMPTINESS AND DISCRETENESS

The closer we get to the view of emptiness, the more we develop a natural respect for the precision of the relative world. Things are at once empty and discrete. Space and order, emptiness and fullness coexist. Things are unproduced yet varied in their manifestation. Phenomena—essentially uncompounded—appear vividly to the senses. Things arise precisely and in order yet are unfindable: An unfindable apple tree always follows an unfindable apple seed. A pear tree never emerges from an apple seed. A banana tree never emerges from a rock. This speaks of the magical relationship of emptiness and discreteness. It is a mistake of ordinary dualistic mind to think that things must be "real" or "solid" in order to function.

People often fear that the realization of emptiness will undermine their ability to function in the world. On the contrary! Why would a mind less impeded by ignorance function less accurately? We have to deal with life as it comes to us. We exit the train station in Old Delhi. All the ricksha and taxi drivers rush at us. . . . We have to pull it together, know where we're going! Don't wander out like a bewildered tourist, dazed and confused. Emptiness doesn't conflict with experience. The ricksha drivers are there, waiting to play the game. Go out, bargain, and get the best rate!

16

Light Comes Through

Potential and Entirety

When the Buddha attained enlightenment under the Bodhi tree, he found the awakened mind to be so subtle, profound, and beyond all expression that he resolved to simply rest in his realization, thinking no one could possibly understand. Aware of his accomplishment, Brahma and Indra requested the Buddha to teach and share his realization with others. Recognizing this request as an auspicious indication of beings' ability or potential to experience what he himself had discovered, the Buddha spoke to this potential, which he knew resided within all beings.

Our buddha potential, which reveals itself to us in unexpected and poignant ways—in ways we can easily identify—is an indication of who we are in our entirety. It expresses itself in our longing for happiness and freedom from suffering and in our search for meaning. We bump up against it when we know something is just not quite right—for instance, when we try so hard to hold on to permanence in the midst of our constantly changing world. It manifests as the intelligence that investigates ignorance and that knows how to distinguish positive actions from negative ones. It sees the difference between selfishness and compassion, and exposes itself in the mind's very ability to recognize and feel touched by truthfulness. We may not directly perceive the hidden source of all this expression, and we may not know the causes and conditions that produce suffering or happiness, but the fact that we long for meaning and goodness is light coming through.

A Fully Illuminated Mind

What is this light that comes through? It is the knowing aspect of the nature of emptiness. On the path, this knowing aspect manifests as our natural intelligence and is basic to everything we experience; in its entirety, it is fully illuminated, unobstructed, pure knowing—Buddhahood. But don't misunderstand; it is not a thing: It is timeless and unfindable in its emptiness. The union of pure knowing and *mahashunyata* is the nature of mind and provides the power for all experience to manifest.*

The nature of mind is always in its entirety. It doesn't get brighter, cleaner, or more fascinating than it already is. There is nothing to clear away or purify, there is nothing to add or improve; the nature is complete. It doesn't create phenomena, nor does it destroy them. It is the nature of all things, and its unobstructed openness functions to simply accommodate and know everything that arises.

Because the nature of mind is intrinsic to who we are—because it is always right in front of us—there is no need to pursue enlightenment or reject pain. There is no need to cling to bliss and happiness or to suppress rough unwanted experiences. These are the activities of confused mind. The essence of all

---

Mahashunyata, literally, "great emptiness." Emptiness provides the space for everything to arise. Its knowing aspect is the source of all that can arise.

Buddhist practice aims at turning away from confusion and toward our own nature—our own potential. Practice becomes simply bringing the mind back to its source, rather than fixing on an external view or fantasy. In this way, Buddhahood is nothing more than a completely unobstructed experience of the nature of our own mind. Isn't it amazing we have this potential! It is present in all our experience. We just need to recognize and trust in it.

RECOMMENDED READING

Dzogchen Ponlop Rinpoche. *Mind Beyond Death*. Ithaca, N.Y.: Snow Lion Publications, 2007.

Dzongsar Khyentse Rinpoche. *What Makes You Not a Buddhist*. Boston: Shambhala Publications, 2007.

Patrul Rinpoche. *The Words of My Pefect Teacher*. Boston: Shambhala Publications, 1998.

Pema Chödrön. *When Things Fall Apart*. Boston: Shambhala Publications, 2000.

Thich Nhat Hanh. *Old Path White Clouds*. Berkeley, Calif.: Parallax Press, 1991.

MANGALA SHRI BHUTI CENTERS

Mangala Shri Bhuti is a nonprofit Tibetan Buddhist organization under the direction of Venerable Dzigar Kongtrül Rinpoche. Mangala Shri Bhuti offers programs on introductory and advanced Buddhist topics by Dzigar Kongtrül Rinpoche and other lineage holders.

Mangala Shri Bhuti has two main centers for study, contemplation, and meditation, Phuntsok Chöling, near Boulder, Colorado, and Pema Ösel Do Ngak Chöling in Vershire, Vermont. Mangalam Dharma Centers, which are groups of students of Dzigar Kongtrül Rinpoche who live in urban centers and gather to support each others' study and practice, exist in New York City, Montreal, the Bay Area, Kyoto, Taipei, and in Bhutan.

If you would like more information about Mangala Shri Bhuti, Dzigar Kongtrül Rinpoche's teaching schedule, or the collection of recorded teachings by Rinpoche available on MP3 CD; or if you would like to visit one of Mangala Shri Bhuti's centers or contact one of the Mangalam Dharma Centers, please use the contact information below, or visit Mangala Shri Bhuti's website, www.mangalashribhuti.org.

In Colorado:
Mangala Shri Bhuti
P.O. Box 4088
Boulder, CO 80306
(303) 459-0184

In Vermont:
Pema Ösel Do Ngak Chöling
Study, Contemplation, and
Meditation Center
322 Eastman Crossroad
Vershire, VT 05079
(802) 333-4521